Lezleigh Ann Bignami

D1578749

HAWAI'IAN
VANILLA
COOKBOOK

Everything Vanilla

outskirts
press

PREFACE

Aloha from the most isolated and beautiful islands in the world. We say, "Lucky we stay Hawai'i nei!" And that is exactly what we truly are, lucky, and we love to share the Aloha in so many ways, especially through our amazing food. This cookbook is exactly that, as Hawai'i fuses together multiple nationalities of people, food, and cultures with respect for one another living together side by side in the same neighborhood. Though we are the fiftieth state, we couldn't be more different and unique in every way. We have our own culture, language, dance, music, religion, food, style, almost everything.

I fuse together my childhood experience in family restaurants, my early years in New Mexico, and my blessed forty-eight-plus years of living in Hawai'i, combined with my culinary studies and experiences in Europe, where I worked in conjunction with a premiere European travel and gourmet magazine *Der Feinschmecker*. I've brought together many influences from around the globe to my recipes, all with the very special ingredient of Hawai'ian Madagascar vanilla.

Culinary creativity is about combining flavors to create harmonious layers, toward the delicious end result: sweet, salty, sour, bitter, umami. You'll notice most of these recipes are savory, my personal approach, and it's my journey through the healing power of vanilla, though I've included some favorite sweet vanilla treats too. We all know and love the sweet application, but I want to introduce to you something very different and very special: savory vanilla.

Hawai'i has a very important lesson for the world: the multiethnic makeup of Hawai'i, the people, and cultures from around the world, living peacefully together and specifically the Hawai'ian culture. I've gratefully lived here most of my life and had the opportunity to travel to many islands throughout the world. Hawai'i doesn't even feel like being in the United States. I've had the privilege—and it is a privilege, not a right—to live here most of my life, raising my son, Michael Koa, so Aloha, gentle, kind, and proud, as keiki o ka'aina (child of the land) with the utmost respect for life and Hawai'i nei. I wish to share some of my kau kau ma'na'o (my food ideas), that is, my recipes with you.

I've incorporated the amazing blessing of vanilla into my recipes in this book for the deep love of vanilla that my son at the age of two and a half introduced to me. I was a confirmed chocoholic from birth (I jest that I was sent to the vanilla farm for vanilla rehab, but it's sort of for real!); therefore, I never understood the haunting allure of vanilla. I was shocked at this sweet little blue-eyed boy, who when asked what flavor ice cream, shave ice, cake, or whatever, he wanted, he'd stomp his foot saying, "No icky chocoit, I want nilla!!!"

Huh? "Are you sure, sweetheart, they've got all different kinds of chocolate?"

"No, Momma, nilla!"

Okay then. It still took me decades to understand his young infinite right-on wisdom with his discerning mature palate—however confounding it was me at that time—of the ever-precious loving, healing vanilla. So here I am now to share with you, "No, Momma, nilla!" recipes. Enjoy and bon appétit!

DEDICATION

This book is lovingly dedicated to the love of my life, my son, Michael Koa, who, I always told from birth, that I aspired to be more like him, that I loved him more than life itself, and I would cease to exist without him. His outstanding talents in music and the arts were in his blood from birth and came naturally for him. And for my dear mother, Peggie Marie, for whom without I would not exist at all.

As I write this book, May 1, 2022, it would have been her ninety-sixth birthday, but she got her wings a few days earlier and is now laughing, dancing, and playing music with her only grandson, my son, surely in heaven. My Guardian Angels.

They both adored my style of cooking, and we thoroughly enjoyed spending countless hours together in the kitchen, cooking and experimenting, with them always encouraging me to write this book, which has taken me years and many bends in the road.

After living on O'ahu for thirty-five-plus years working in orthopedics, I moved to the Big Island in 2009 to build a house for my son. Building it as a single woman in Volcano was quite a feat and an experience! My son and mother came to visit in 2011 to check out his little house.

In 2018, I became a volcano refugee fleeing from an historic eruption of Kilauea of Mauna Loa, where the little house I had built for my son had between five hundred to seven hundred earthquakes a day. What seemed to be an ongoing nightmare at the time became my saving grace.

Surviving historic hurricanes and a volcano eruption, multiple surgeries, and auto accidents, along with two deadly bacterial infections was nothing compared to the sudden heartbreaking passing of my only child. The only grandson and nephew on either side, my beloved son at the tender age of twenty-five years old. It was surly Takotsubo cardiomyopathy, and it was devastating. I couldn't bring myself to speak of the unspeakable. I wouldn't let my brain and heart communicate, for it's a mother's worst nightmare. I was totally and completely broken.

Mio Michelangelo. You only get through it; you never get over it. I felt I couldn't survive it, day in and day out, by myself in the gloomy volcanic rainforest jungle. I'm certain it was him, guiding me out of it, even if it took the world's largest active volcano to follow an unforeseen path and to the healing powers of vanilla, restoring my culinary inspirations and creations, my music, and beyond, that has been a huge part of my healing. Let vanilla embrace and love you too.

Yes, these pages are lovingly dedicated to both of them. Aloha nui loa, a'hui hou no kakou, much love until we meet again.

I'd also like to acknowledge many longtime dear friends, who supported and believed in me. There are too many to name; you know who you are. To Janice, who helped me get this work finally published, and big thanks from the bottom of my heart to so many of my dear friends and family who have contributed to my life and held me up when I couldn't see the light of day. I am so very grateful for all of you. There is a family of origin and then there's truly a family of choice. To our dear brother Scott. Huge hugs to each and every one of you.

And to The Vanillerie and staff in Kailua-Kona, Hawai'i, for allowing me the amazing healing experience of being amongst the vanilla and to share its stunning beauty and incredible story with visitors and locals alike. Vanilla can be a treatment for antianxiety, an antioxidant, it has anti aging properties, a mild antidepressant, an anti-inflammatory, and an aphrodisiac, as well as an exotic perfume on top of being the most beloved flavor in the world! Indulge yourself every day in vanilla, incorporate vitamin "V" into your daily healthy vitamin regime, and make your own extract!

I have long been influenced by Julia Child. She was the reason for my first trip to Paris, and it took me three more visits to begin to understand Paris. You see, I was the weird kid who raced home after school, not to watch cartoons or Sesame Street, but to see Julia. Always an inspiration. I even got to shop at her favorite neighborhood market in Cambridge, Massachusetts. After my studies at the University of Hawai'i in physical education and music, I was accepted to Berklee School of Music in Boston, to further my study as a jazz vocalist. Oh, I've had quite a lifetime—it seems like more than a hundred of them! And I am grateful for them all.

Ironically, years later, I was proposed to in Paris on Valentine's Day and married in a quaint little chapel in Stein on Rhine in Switzerland, on the Bodensee. The ceremony was completed with a yodeling choir from the rafters and a two-day Oktoberfest party attended by some of Europe's finest chefs, who absolutely loved my Hawai'ian influence into their European cuisine! Yup, another one of my lifetimes!

Peace be with you, while I head into the next chapter of my life. I wish you good health with vanilla! Aloha, always, L

PREPARATION FOR THIS BOOK

A few necessities to begin:

Vanilla pods

This is to make your own extract (*Vanilla Extract recipe)

(*Vanilla extract recipe using a 40%–80%-proof descent alcohol for extraction. Glycerin can be substituted for alcohol, personal choice)

(Or buy a good brand of extract. Check the label though. It's hard to find the proper ratio of extract, which is 1 lb. vanilla to 1 gallon of alcohol. It's almost impossible to find in the US. I only know of a few companies other than the Vanillerie.)

Vanilla caviar

Vanilla powder

Vanilla salt, pepper, and sugar

It's preferable to make your own Vanilla Extract,* because most commercial brands (no matter how much you pay for it) are either watered down, made with a rot-your-gut alcohol for extraction, or have unnecessary added preservatives and sugar. The flavor ends up being incongruent with the aroma; it smells good, but it doesn't taste good until you cook it off. There is no real clear vanilla extract.

As stated above, there are only two ingredients in vanilla extract, vanilla and alcohol, period. Sourcing your own vanilla from an ethically sourced grower is the way to go, and when doing that, make sure the beans are soft and supple. That also goes for the caviar; the vanilla caviar is the deep rich gooey sticky black center of the churned pod. Vanilla paste is made with just the caviar and agave (thirty beans to 1 cup). Vanilla powder is made from dried pods after you've made your extract. It's also the way to make the vanilla salt, pepper, and sugar that you'll need for the recipes in this book. In the interim, you can use a good extract, a little drop in pepper and mix it with salt and sugar.

I highly recommend purchasing the DIY Vanilla Extract Kit from The Vanillerie in Kailua-Kona, Hawai'i, either by visiting personally or online. They grow the very best Hawai'ian Madagascar vanilla beans, with a deep rich buttery flavor, cultivated in the lush Hawai'ian volcanic cinder and exquisite Big Island climate, possibly creating the very tastiest vanilla on the planet!

All vanilla originates in Mexico (and is a hermaphrodite) which has a midrange flavor with a smoky quality. The two hybrids are Tahitian and Madagascar. Tahitian vanilla is light and floral and is considered French vanilla. Madagascar vanilla, as I stated previously, has a deep buttery quality and is considered bourbon vanilla.

Most people don't understand the intensity of the production of this precious fruit that we totally take for granted. It is the love plant for sure, with the long, deep green vines, reaching out to embrace, clinging to each other, caressing, intertwining intimately. In Hawai'ian, it's called honi honi; they are hugging and kissing each other. It makes sense in view of the heart-wrenching Totonacs legend (Vera Cruz, Mexico) where the precious vanilla sprang forth from the blood of two lovers. I truly believe it is the fruit of the gods and goddesses, that we mere mortals get to enjoy, and my hope is that we will appreciate and respect it, too, like my Michael Koa did as a toddler. It took me so much longer!

It takes four to five years from the precious baby shoot of the vanilla orchid vine to a divine bottle of extract—three years from new shoot to bloom. Thus, obtaining your own vanilla pods is the way to go, for real vanilla hits over 250 taste sensors on your palette with over 300 flavor compounds; the imitation vanilla hits two! Therefore, the statement "plain as vanilla" could not be less true; it's very complex and very sophisticated.

The United States is the largest importer of vanilla, second only to France (basically where the sweet application originated), but unfortunately, 80 percent of the vanilla that is found in our food is imitation. Demand the best, and if you make it yourself, it will be the best extract you've ever tasted. It's delicious right out of the bottle; you can use it raw.

*Vanilla Extract

8–9 medium-sized vanilla pods

10 oz. 40%–80%-proof alcohol (vodka, rum, bourbon, etc.)

Clean 10 oz. glass bottle with tight-fitting lid or cork

Score the vanilla pods lengthwise with the back of a butter knife to expose the caviar; be careful not to cut all the way through. Keeping it intact, cut it with scissors crosswise into ½-inch pieces. Place all the little pieces in the bottom of the bottle and fill it with the alcohol of your choice, no stronger than 40%–80% proof, or it will burn the precious pods. Seal it tightly, put the bottle into a cool, dark place, and leave it for 3–4 months or until it develops a deep brown color, turning the bottle to marry it every week or so. Designate the bottle of alcohol because you'll be doing this for at least a year and a half, if not the rest of your life and you don't want to mix alcohols that will muddy the extract.

If you do not wish to use alcohol, it's possible to extract it with glycerin.

I have five DIY kits going at the same time for different testings of this cookbook. The first one is in vodka, which is odorless and tasteless and allows the vanilla to bloom through. The second is in bourbon, and with the bourbon vanilla, they totally love each other! The third is in rum, which extracts the fastest. The fourth is in cognac, my personal favorite. The fifth one I'm making in conjunction with friends in Switzerland is a pear (Williams Pear) schnapps liqueur. Oh la la, I can't wait for that one! By the way, no need for expensive alcohols, Costco rules!

Once the extract is a nice brown color, turn the bottle to marry it together, mixing it well, and pour off the top 2 oz. into a separate small bottle. That portion goes into your pantry for the recipes in this book. Then fill the large bottle back up again with your alcohol of choice, the same as the one you began with. You can repeat this process three to four times or until the extract is no longer brown, basically turning into a vanilla cocktail. At that point, you can enjoy it that way or either continue to make extract by recharging it with fresh pods or you can remove the bits and pieces, dry them, and grind them in a coffee grinder to make your vanilla powder, salt, pepper, and sugar! And start another extract kit! Always be sure to use Kona Hawai'ian salt in these recipes.

The following recipes are some of our favorites, and all of them call for vanilla. Whether it states vanilla or Hawai'ian vanilla, it is always pure vanilla, no imitations here (no clear extract; it's not real). The proper ratio for extract is 1 lb. vanilla to 1 gallon of alcohol. This is pretty difficult to find; thus, I suggest you source it from The Vanillerie, and if not, a reputable source of Madagascar vanilla pods. Again, in this book, you'll be using vanilla extract, vanilla caviar (the thick gooney center of the pod), vanilla powder, vanilla sugar, salt, and pepper. If you're able to source it locally, by all means do so. While you're making your vanilla extract kit, which will ultimately be your source for the vanilla ingredients stated above, in the interim you can use your own sourced pods to create these ingredients:

Vanilla extract = 8 vanilla pods and 8–12 oz. 40%–80% proof
Vanilla caviar = the inside of the pod.
Vanilla sugar, salt, and pepper = dried pods, ground up and added to it.

Bon viva la vanilla appetit! Watch for the next upcoming vanilla cookbook! www.hawaiianvanillacookbook.com

CONTENTS

Desserts

Our Furry K9 Friends

Vanilla Cocktails

VANILLA

BEAUTIFUL BIG ISLAND, HAWAI'I

BREAKFAST HAWAI'IAN VANILLA STYLE

VANILLA BANANA PANCAKES

VANILLA BANANA PANCAKES

- I cup flour
- I cup milk
- 2 teaspoons baking powder
- ¼ teaspoon vanilla salt
- 2 tablespoon vanilla sugar
- I large egg, plus I egg white, separated
- 2 tablespoons melted butter
- I tablespoon vegetable oil
- I teaspoon vanilla extract
- I teaspoon vanilla caviar
- I banana, sliced
- Powdered sugar and honey, for garnish

Lightly grease and heat a skillet. In a medium bowl, combine the dry ingredients and set aside. In a separate medium bowl, blend together milk, 1 egg yolk, butter, vanilla extract, and vanilla caviar. In a separate bowl, whisk together the egg whites until stiff. Bring together the dry and wet ingredients and mix lightly, then gently fold in the egg whites. Pour batter onto a medium-heated skillet. When it starts to bubble on top, lay sliced banana on top and turn over. Cook until golden brown. Dust with powdered sugar or honey.

This is a Lililha Bakery delight, the fluffiest pancakes ever. As I'd watch them and experiment to get them as fluffy and light as theirs, it was like with their waffles; it's the stiff egg whites that did the trick!

Protein: 14% 41kcal. Fat: 49% 145 kcal. Carbs: 38% 112 kcal

VANILLA WAFFLES

- 1 cup flour
- 2 tablespoons sugar
- 1 teaspoon baking powder
- ¼ teaspoon vanilla salt
- 2 large eggs, separated
- 1 cup milk
- 1 teaspoon vanilla extract
- 1 teaspoon vanilla caviar
- 4 tablespoon melted butter
- Coconut, lilikoi (passion fruit), maple, or whatever type syrup

Lightly oil and heat a waffle iron (according to manufacturer's instructions). Mix the dry ingredients in a large bowl. In a separate bowl, whip the egg whites until stiff, set aside. In another bowl, combine milk, egg yolks, vanilla extract and caviar, and then add the dry ingredients. Once it has come together, gently fold in the egg whites. Pour batter in the center of the waffle iron, not too much to make it flow out of the iron once the cover is closed, and cook per manufacturer's instructions until the waffle is golden brown on both sides. Enjoy with your favorite syrup or fresh fruit, pineapple, mango, berries, etc. powdered sugar, or whipped cream.

Late at night after singing in Waikiki, the band and I would head to our favorite place, Liliha Bakery, a twenty-four-hour a day joy! They make the absolute best pancakes and waffles. I'd sit at the counter watching carefully how they accomplished this amazing feat. Back at my own kitchen, I'd work it over and over and finally figured it out! Enjoy it with your loved ones. I do!

Protein: 12% 41kcal. Fat: 50% 165 kcal. Carbs: 38% 127kcal.

VANILLA MAUI ONION MARMALADE AND EGGS AND CORNED BEEF

- ¼ cup chopped onion
- 1 can corned beef for three people (Replace with charred portabellas for vegan)
- 1 teaspoon vanilla caviar
- 2 eggs per person
- Rice, potatoes, or English muffin for side

MAUI ONION MARMALADE
- 2 cups chopped Maui onion tablespoons butter
- 1 teaspoon oil
- 2 teaspoons butter, melted
- 1 tablespoon vanilla extract
- 1 teaspoon vanilla salt and pepper to taste

Sauté onions in a little oil in a nonstick pan on medium heat. Once browned, add the corned beef, and cook until it is thoroughly combined, then add the vanilla caviar. Set aside.

For the Marmalade, melt butter and oil in a skillet, add Maui onions, sauté on medium heat until browned, add vanilla extract, salt, and pepper. Set aside.

Poach or fry sunny side up eggs. Plate corned beef, place eggs on top, side with rice, potatoes, or English muffin. Top with Maui onion marmalade.

Protein: 21% 99 kcal. Fat: 51% 235 kcal. Carbs: 28% 130 kcal

A honeymoon breakfast in Hana, Maui. A breakfast to remember...

THE 5 MOTHER SAUCES—
HAWAI'IAN VANILLA STYLE

5 VANILLA MOTHER SAUCES

THE 5 (VANILLA) MOTHER SAUCES AND BEURRE BLANC

HAWAI'IAN VANILLA STYLE

The five French Mother sauces are: hollandaise, béchamel, velouté, espagnole, and tomat. All are made with a roux, except hollandaise. Roux is equal parts fat and flour sautéed together to create different variations of thickening. These five sauces are a Godsend to anyone interested in the kitchen, each one its own particular use, though no boundaries. We'll be using them in this book and, hopefully, beyond in your own culinary creations. Learn these five sauces and you'll open the door to beaucoup recipes from around the globe, not just the sweet little unassuming French menus!

Here are the 5 Vanilla Mother Sauces, Hawai'ian style

Hollandaise is the one without a roux. It's an emulsified butter and egg yolk combination, much like mayonnaise, which is also the emulsification of oil and eggs, so you want to keep it moving. Vanilla hollandaise is an included recipe under Vanilla Eggs Benedict, so we'll move on to béchamel.

Start with Hawai'ian vanilla roux: Melt 4 tablespoons butter in sauté pan, add 2 teaspoons vanilla, ½ teaspoon vanilla caviar, and 4 tablespoons flour. Cook at medium heat until the flour taste is cooked out, whisking for a couple of minutes. Add vanilla salt and pepper to taste (easy on those; it'll be added and balanced later).

There are different levels of roux, depending on how much you brown this basic recipe. You don't want to burn it, but you definitely need to cook it down. Once you have it, just add…

2nd is béchamel: a roux thinned with milk or cream (pretty bland on its own) as the base. However, it's the start of many well-known favorites, like mac 'n' cheese, potatoes au gratin, etc. Make roux and add cheese! Wow! Like the Vanilla Mac 'n' Cheese* recipe included in this book.

3rd is velouté: a "velvety" cream sauce of roux and thinned down with chicken or fish stock. Obviously for chicken or fish.

4th is espagnole: a dark one that starts with a mirepoix, (sautéed onions, celery, carrots) cooked down and thickened with a browned roux with thinning down with beef or veal stock. For beef and meat.

5th is tomat: this one we all know and love; simply tomatoes cooked down and thickened with a roux and thinned down with vegetable or pork stock.

Beurre blanc: the bonus sauce for poached fish and seafood.

- 2 medium shallots, minced
- 1½ cups white wine
- ½ cup white wine or champagne vinegar
- 1 cup butter
- 1 tablespoon vanilla extract
- 1 teaspoon vanilla caviar
- Vanilla salt and pepper to taste
- Fresh green herbs, chives, tarragon, etc.

Sauté shallots in wine and vinegar, bring to a boil, reduce to medium, and simmer until liquid is reduced to about 2 tablespoons, about 10 minutes. Turn heat to lowest setting and whisk in butter 1 tablespoon at a time into shallot mixture. Allow each one to melt before adding the next. Add vanilla extract and caviar and keep it low heat and don't allow it to get hot. Season with vanilla salt and pepper. Garnish with herbs, and serve over fish and seafood.

One of my favorite beurre blanc dishes was surprisingly discovered in a seaside café in Brittany, where you can buy seafood by the meter. With a nice fresh filet of fish over a bed of sauerkraut, you've got to try it. It's amazing! Michael loved this unusual combination.

So, see how easy it can be? It's not so difficult at all. It just takes practice with a clean palate and open olfactory senses to be all about the taste and smell of them individually.

Cooking is about combining a pleasant palette of flavors, creating harmonious layers appealing to our eyes, nose, and even our ears, before it hits our lips. Including all the components of sweet, sour, bitter, salty, umami, then layering in spices, freshness, color, contrast, etc. A recipe could be one hundred ingredients or maybe just three: KISS. You be the master of your own culinary path. Enjoy it and share the joy! Aloha nui loa.

APPETIZERS/PU'PU

VANILLA HAWAI'IAN AHI POKE

VANILLA HAWAI'IAN AHI POKE

- 1 lb. fresh sushi-grade ahi tuna, cubed into ¾ inch
- ¼ cup shoyu (soy sauce)
- 1 tablespoon vanilla extract
- 1 teaspoon vanilla caviar
- 2 tablespoons sesame oil
- 2 teaspoons fresh grated ginger
- ½ cup chopped scallions (reserve some for garnish)
- 2 tablespoons chopped roasted unsalted macadamia nuts
- 2 tablespoons crushed red pepper flakes
- 1 teaspoon vanilla salt to taste
- 1 teaspoon toasted sesame seeds
- Dash of fresh lemon or lime juice and zest
- Dried seaweed, optional

Whisk shoyu, vanilla extract and caviar, sesame oil, ginger, scallions, macadamia nuts, pepper flakes, and salt in a bowl. Place cubed tuna in the bowl and marinade covered in the fridge for 2 hours. Gently mix again and top with toasted sesame, remaining scallions, and a squeeze of lemon or lime and zest.

Enjoy! Of course, this is an absolute must for us in Hawai'i; we gotta have it! We eat it with a side of plain rice or poi, and you must try it! We eat it for special occasions like luaus or parties or when we just want to simply treat ourselves.

Protein: 45% 93kcal. Fat: 47% 96 kcal. Carbs: 8% 16kcal

VANILLA GUACAMOLE

- 2 ripe avocados
- 1–2 finely chopped tomatoes
- ¼ cup finely chopped cilantro
- 1 finely chopped jalapeno
- ¼ cup finely chopped onions
- 1 tablespoon vanilla extract
- 1 teaspoon vanilla caviar
- 2–3 teaspoons fresh lime juice and zest
- Vanilla salt and pepper to taste

Peel avocados and mash with a fork (or a molcajete if you have one) until it is smashed with texture. Add the rest of the ingredients, except the lime juice, and gently mix. Add the lime juice, salt, and pepper to taste. Enjoy with tortilla, on toast, or taro chips! Eat for breakfast, lunch, dinner, or a snack. So good for you anytime!

Protein: 5% 8 kcal. Fat: 71% 124 kcal. Carbs 24% 42 kcal

LUNCH AND BRUNCH

VANILLA EGGS BENEDICT

VANILLA EGGS BENEDICT

Serves 4

HOLLANDAISE:
- ¾ cup butter
- 4 large egg yolks
- 2 teaspoons fresh lemon juice, to taste
- 1½ teaspoons vanilla extract
- ¼ teaspoon cayenne pepper
- ½ teaspoon vanilla salt and pepper
- 1½ teaspoon vanilla caviar

POACHED EGGS:
- 2 tablespoons vinegar
- 8 large eggs

FOR ASSEMBLY:
- 4 English muffins, split and toasted
- 8 slices Canadian bacon, lox, or lobster
- Hawaiian vanilla salt and white pepper to taste
- Chives and parsley for garnish

To make the hollandaise, melt the butter. Place the egg yolks in the blender with 1 teaspoon of water. Use the quick pulse until it is blended, a few seconds. Heat the butter until it bubbles but before it browns. With the blender on low, slowly pour the bubbling butter into the blender. It will begin to incorporate and thicken. If too thick add a little more butter, if too thin keep blending. Add the lemon, vanilla extract, cayenne, salt and pepper to taste. Gently fold in the vanilla caviar. Cover the sauce with plastic wrap to discourage a skin to form, and set aside.

POACHING EGGS:

Fill a medium skillet with 3 inches of water, add vinegar, and bring to a simmer. Put eggs (2–3 at a time) into a measuring cup and stir the water in a clockwise motion, slowly pour eggs into the center and let them swirl around, enveloping the whites around the yolk. Check the eggs at four minutes with a slotted spoon for firmness of the whites, with yolk runny. If not done, allow another minute. Remove from the water and allow it to drain on a plate lined with a clean cloth kitchen towel. Set aside and begin assembly.

Begin plating with toasted English muffin half. Place bacon, lox, or lobster on it, then place the poached egg and top with the hollandaise. Garnish with chives or parsley.

Don't let this recipe intimidate you! I've basically been mandated by friends and family for decades to make this for most holidays. With the addition of vanilla, it's a game changer, makes it even more special! Bon appetit!

Protein: 15% 110 kcal. Fat 71% 528 kcal. Carbs: 15% 109 kcal

VANILLA FRITTATA

- 6 large eggs
- ¼ cup heavy cream
- ½ teaspoon vanilla salt
- ½ teaspoon vanilla pepper
- 1 teaspoon vanilla extract
- 1 teaspoon vanilla caviar
- 1 cup shredded cheese
- 2 cups of add-ins*

Preheat the oven to 350 F degrees, and oil a 10-inch greased (oven proof) skillet. In a large bowl, whisk together eggs, cream, salt, pepper, vanilla extract and caviar and fold in cheese. Once you've decided on add-ins, stir them into this mixture, pour it into the skillet, and place the skillet in the preheated oven. Bake uncovered for 10 to 15 minutes, or until the eggs have set in the center.

*ADD-INS:

These can be a whole array of your favorite things, whether raw or sautéed. For example, a Mexican one with red and green chilis, onions and cheese, or sautéed veggies. It can be Italian with pizza ingredients or Chinese with stir-fry. Let your imagination run wild, and create something different, like Hawai'ian pineapple and ham. Make enough for 2 cups of add-ins.

Protein: 29% 93 kcal. Fat: 69% 218 kcal. Carbs: 2% 6 kcal

VANILLA MARGUERITE PIZZA

VANILLA MARGUERITE PIZZA

DOUGH:

- 4 cups flour, divided
- 1 ½ cups water, room temp
- 1 package of active yeast
- 1 teaspoon vanilla salt

TOPPING:

- ½ lb. mozzarella, in small pieces
- 2 cups fresh tomatoes, peeled
- Fresh bunch of basil
- Extra virgin olive oil
- 2 teaspoons vanilla extract
- 1 tablespoon vanilla caviar
- Vanilla salt and pepper to taste

Begin with making the dough. Dissolve the yeast in the room temperature water. Once dissolved, add half the flour, mix quickly, and cover with a damp cloth. Let it rest for 30 minutes. Then add the rest of the flour and vanilla salt. Knead the dough vigorously for at least 10 minutes. Shape the dough into a ball and place in a bowl, cover with plastic wrap, and refrigerate for 24 hours. Remove the dough from the fridge and allow it to come to room temperature, about 2 hours. Stretch out the dough using your fingertips to extend to the shape of your pizza pan, about 13 x 15 inches. Cover and let it rest for 30 minutes before baking.

In the meantime, preheat the oven to 450 F degrees, and in a bowl break up the peeled tomatoes with a fork, add salt, vanilla extract, and vanilla caviar. Once the dough has rested, add the tomato mixture to the top of the pizza dough and place it on the bottom rack of the oven. Bake for the first 5 minutes, then move to the middle rack for another 7 to 10 minutes, or until the crust is golden brown. Remove from the oven. Immediately add mozzarella and top with pieces of hand-torn fresh basil, then drizzle with olive oil and serve.

Viva la Italia, mio amora pizza Margherita! Pizza was always on my birthday dinner wish list as a kid, and going to its birthplace had me in heaven! In Roma, I stuffed it into all of my pockets before catching the midnight train with a humorous story of an unsuspecting train conductor discovering it! Viva la pizza! Try this simple blissful one, especially with a delicious thin crust and simple fresh basil–tomato topping. Enjoy it with family and friends! Buon appetito!

Protein: 23% 126 kcal. Fat: 2% 12 kcal. Carbs: 75% 411 kcal

VANILLA WATERMELON LILIKOI GAZPACHO

- 3 medium ripe tomatoes, chopped
- 3 cups cubed watermelon
- 1 English cucumber, chopped
- 1 green bell pepper, chopped
- 1 rib celery with leaves, chopped
- 2 tablespoons fresh ginger root, grated
- 2 tablespoons dry red chili pepper
- Juice of 2 fresh limes
- 1 fresh passion fruit (lilikoi), just fruit and seeds inside
- Bunch of fresh basil
- ½ small white onion, chopped
- 1 clove garlic, crushed
- 1 tablespoon vanilla caviar
- 2 teaspoons vanilla extract
- ¼ cup extra virgin olive oil
- Splash of champagne vinegar or sherry vinegar
- Pinch vanilla salt and pepper
- Sour cream for garnish
- Roasted macadamia nuts for garnish

Wash and dry all the vegetables, setting a few of each aside for garnish, and putting all the rest of the ingredients in the blender. Pulse until blended to chopped soupy consistency. Add vanilla salt and pepper to taste. Refrigerate for 2 hours and serve in chilled bowls. Garnish with remaining veggies, a dab of sour cream, and sprinkle of macadamia nuts.

Serve with a toasted garlic baguette! Yummy!

Protein: 10% 5 kcal. Fat: 6% 3 kcal. Carbs: 85% 44 kcal

VANILLA BOUILLABAISSE

- 2 quarts water
- 2 tablespoons salt
- Fish heads, shrimp shells, clam and fish stock (from the scrapes of
- the seafood below)
- 2 cups leeks, chopped
- 2 cups onions, chopped
- ½ cup olive oil
- 6 cups fresh tomatoes
- 4–5 cloves fresh garlic
- Sprigs of fresh basil
- Sprigs of fresh parsley
- Sprigs of fresh thyme
- ¼ cup chopped fresh fennel
- 2 bay leaves
- Fresh orange peel
- 5 strands of saffron
- 2 tablespoons vanilla caviar
- 1 tablespoon vanilla extract
- 4 cups of eight varieties of fresh lean fish, such as ono, mahi mahi, halibut, flounder, bass, etc. And shellfish such as scallops, lobster, shrimp, mussels, clams, etc.
- Vanilla salt and pepper to taste

In a large pot, add the water, salt, fish heads, shrimp shells, and clam stock to create the stock. Combine all the ingredients except the fish and vanilla. Simmer for 40 minutes and strain, then add the vanilla caviar and extract. First add in the firm fish, cut in large chunks, and cook for 10 minutes. Add the shellfish last, and cook for 5 minutes. Add the vanilla salt and pepper to taste. Serve with a toasted baguette and bon appetit!

This is one of our favorites that I learned in Provence, where we used to spend the summers and always a winter trip for truffle season, where the air was permeated with truffles in the winter and lavender in the summer! My son had a young, very well-developed refined palate, and we so cherished all these adventures. We mostly stayed at a special pretty little hotel with an amazing chef who would bring special treats from the kitchen to spoil him. Though there are similar recipes re-created in different parts of the world, this is basically the one. Merci beaucoup, France!

Protein:3% 6 kcal. Fat: 74% 162 kcal. Carbs: 23% 51 kcal

VANILLA LOCO MOCO

VANILLA LOCO MOCO

Serve 4

- 1½ lb. ground angus beef or turkey
- 2 tablespoons chopped onion
- 1 tablespoon crushed garlic
- 1 teaspoon Worcestershire
- 1 tablespoon olive oil, plus more for brushing
- 1 tablespoon butter
- 2 teaspoons vanilla extract
- 1 tablespoon vanilla caviar
- Vanilla salt and pepper to taste
- 4 eggs, fried or poached
- 4 tablespoons flour
- 3 tablespoons butter to equal 4 tablespoons of pan drippings
- ½ cup room temperature milk to thin roux

Lightly sauté onions and garlic in olive oil and butter in medium heavy skillet, then add the Worcestershire sauce and vanilla extract, and cook until the onions are translucent.

On the side, form the meat into four equal pieces/burgers, gently not to handle it too much, making a depression in the center of each.

In another skillet on medium-high heat, brush the burgers with oil and sear on each side for 3 to 5 minutes (turkey 5 to 7 minutes). Remove the burgers from the pan and set aside.

In the same skillet, make a roux in the drippings by adding flour and butter, cooking completely, to a light brown stage. Add the milk slowly until you achieve a smooth thick gravy consistency and add vanilla caviar and combined sauteed onion and garlic mixture. Plate the burger, pour gravy over it, and top with a fried or poached egg.

This is a local Hawai'ian go-to 24/7, loved by young and old alike, served with a side of rice or potatoes, Ono-licious!

Protein: 35% 226 kcal. Fat 61% 391 kcal. Carbs: 4% 28 kcal

VANILLA QUICHE LOLEINA (LORRAINE)

- 1 9-inch frozen or homemade pie crust
- 6 slices of bacon, cut in pieces
- 4 large eggs, beaten
- 1¼ cups heavy cream
- ½ cup chopped shallots
- 1 tablespoon vanilla extract
- 1 teaspoon vanilla caviar
- ¼ teaspoon vanilla salt
- ¼ teaspoon vanilla pepper ground
- Pinch of nutmeg
- 1¼ cups shredded Gruyere cheese

Preheat the oven to 400 F degrees, and place the rack in the middle of the oven. Pierce a fork in the bottom and sides of the frozen or fresh pie crust, and bake it for 10 minutes or until it is a light golden brown. Set it aside to cool and reduce the oven heat to 325 F degrees.

In a medium saucepan over medium heat, cook the bacon until it's crispy, and then drain it on a paper towel. Pour off all but 1 tablespoon of bacon fat, and add in the chopped shallots. Cook over medium-low heat until they are translucent and soft. Remove the pan from the heat and set aside.

In a medium bowl combine eggs and cream, vanilla extract and caviar, salt, pepper, and nutmeg. Gently fold in the cheese until it is completely combined. Spread the cooked shallots over the bottom of the cooked and cooled pie crust, placing the crust on a baking sheet before pouring the egg cream mixture into it.

Place the quiche on the baking sheet into the oven and bake at 325 for 45 to 50 minutes or until the crust is golden brown and the center has set. Serve with a salad Caprese* and enjoy! Bon appetit!

Protein: 12% 145 kcal. Fat: 64% 791 kcal. Carbs: 25% 309 kcal

SALADS

VANILLA VINAIGRETTE

VANILLA VINAIGRETTE

- 1 cup olive oil
- ¼ cup fresh shallots, finely chopped
- 2 tablespoons Dijon mustard
- ¼ cup wine vinegar
- 2 tablespoons vanilla salt (or more to your liking)
- 1½ teaspoon vanilla caviar
- 2 teaspoon vanilla extract
- 1 teaspoon vanilla pepper

Simply put all ingredients into a food processor, a blender, or in a bowl with an immersion blender until completely pulverized. Taste to adjust salt (should be salty! If not, add more). Pour into a clean glass jar with top and let it set for a few hours. Wonderful.

This is a staple to keep on hand, utilizing it in many different applications. Because of the olive oil, it's not very good to refrigerate it; you can use other lighter oils if you wish. It's a favorite that I use over salads, veggies, chicken, seafood, my fingers?! Taught to me by Madame La'hardion of Vannes, Brittany, France. It is a fond memory of an amazing part of France with incredible seafood everywhere! I was like a pig in mud, from Hawai'i. They sell seafood by the yard or meter and oh my goodness the bouillabaisse is heavenly! The open markets to me and my food brain were like seafood porn! With the ever-pleasant sound of an accordion player in the background, the symphony of crustaceans, fish, snails, and all kinds of sea creatures alighting the market with their colorful scales, shells of beautiful colors, and tasty gastropods in the foreground and flavors that pop. WOW! And it's hard for me to say between Brittany and Provence bouillabaisse, both were unbelievably delicious!

Protein: 5% 1 kcal. Fat: 74% 13 kcal. Carbs: 21% 4 kcal

VANILLA SALAD CAPRESE

VANILLA SALAD CAPRESE

- 9 Large fresh tomatoes, sliced
- 24 oz. fresh mozzarella, sliced
- Bunch of fresh basil
- 6 tablespoons extra virgin vanilla olive oil (+1 teaspoon vanilla extract)
- 1 tablespoon balsamic reduction (cook down 4 tablespoons to 1 tablespoon)
- 2 tablespoons Vanilla Vinaigrette*
- Vanilla salt and pepper to taste

Begin by alternating the slices of tomato and mozzarella in a circle on a platter until you've used all the slices, and then place whole basil leaves between the layers to mimic the colors of the flag of Italy. Drizzle vanilla olive oil and balsamic reduction (sauté balsamic vinegar at low temperature until half of what it was). Finish with the Vanilla Vinaigrette.* Sprinkle with Hawai'ian vanilla salt and serve immediately.

This is a favorite all over Europe, so easy and bright with the fresh basil and tomatoes. Yummy!

*Recipe is in the index.

Protein: 47% 222 kcal. Fat: 39% 184 kcal. Carbs: 14% 66 kcal

VANILLA SALAD NIÇOISE

VANILLA SALAD NIÇOISE

- 3 large heads of Manoa lettuce or bib, washed and dried
- Extra virgin olive oil
- 1½ lbs. fresh green string beans, trimmed, blanched, shocked
- Vanilla Vinaigrette*
- 3–4 ripe Waimea or heirloom tomatoes, sliced
- 8–12 oz. fresh grilled Ahi or water-packed albacore tuna, flaked
- Fresh lemon or lime
- 1 Waimea or English cucumber, sliced
- 1 qt. Hawai'ian Vanilla Potato Salad**
- 8 hard-boiled eggs, cut lengthwise
- 1 can flat anchovy filets in oil, drained
- ½ cup black olives
- 1–4 tablespoons capers
- ¼ cup fresh parsley, minced
- Vanilla salt and pepper to taste

In a large wooden (Koa in Hawai'i) salad bowl or platter lined with whole leaves of lettuce, drizzle with olive oil and sprinkle with vanilla salt.

Toss the beans in a separate bowl with some of the Vanilla Vinaigrette*

Arrange the tomatoes in the center of the lettuce, and drizzle vinaigrette over them. Season the tuna lightly with a squeeze of fresh lemon or lime, placing on top of tomatoes. Arrange the beans in equal intervals around the center, interspersing the cucumber and Hawaiian Vanilla Potato Salad** to create a mandala of sorts, crowning it with the eggs with a curl of anchovy to create a rose shape on top of each egg. Spoon a bit more vinaigrette and sprinkle with olives, capers, and parsley. Eat it fresh! Viva la France!

*Go to index for recipe

Protein: 36% 190 kcal. Fat: 40% 211 kcal. Carbs: 23% 121 kcal

**HAWAIIAN VANILLA POTATO SALAD

- 1½ lbs. warm sliced cooked potatoes in a bowl.

In a separate bowl combine 2 tablespoons chopped shallots, 3 tablespoons chopped celery, 5 tablespoons mayonnaise, 1 teaspoon vanilla caviar, 1 teaspoon vanilla extract, Hawaiian vanilla salt and pepper to taste, ¼ cup chicken stock, 2 tablespoons wine vinegar, 2–3 tablespoons chopped parsley. Toss gently together and adjust seasoning. Pour over the potatoes and toss to cover. Finish with a drizzle of olive oil and chives.

Protein: 27% 64 kcal. Fat: 30% 69 kcal. Carbs: 43% 100 kcal

VANILLA SPICY COLESLAW

VANILLA SPICY COLESLAW

- 3 cups chopped coleslaw combination: cabbage, kale, broccoli stalks, Brussels sprouts, chicory
- I cup fresh mango, cubed
- ¾ cup of mayonnaise
- ¼ cup chopped onions or shallots
- ¼ cup green chili (New Mexican)
- I ½ tablespoons red chili flakes
- I tablespoon garlic powder
- ½ cup cider vinegar
- 4 tablespoons honey or molasses
- I tablespoon vanilla extract
- I teaspoon vanilla caviar
- I tablespoon whole roasted coriander
- I teaspoon whole white vanilla pepper, cracked
- 2 tablespoons chopped ginger root
- Roasted macadamia nuts for garnish

Place chopped slaw mixture in a large bowl and chill.

In a separate bowl, mix together all other ingredients, except for mango, ginger root, and macadamia nuts. Mix well, creating the dressing. Let the mixture stand covered at room temperature for an hour. After an hour, put the mango and ginger root on top of the slaw mixture, pour the dressing over the top, and toss gently. Refrigerate for an hour or longer for best results, but it can be eaten immediately. Garnish with macadamia nuts, if desired.

Protein: 6% 10 kcal. Fat: 50% 88 kcal. Carbs: 4% 76 kcal

VANILLA TABBOULEH

- 2 bunches of fresh parsley, chopped
- I bunch scallions, chopped
- ½ cup fresh mint leaves, chopped
- 3 large ripe tomatoes, diced
- ¼ cup fine bulgur
- ½ cup water
- ¼ cup olive oil
- 2 tablespoons fresh lemon juice and zest
- I tablespoon vanilla caviar
- I tablespoon vanilla extract
- I teaspoon vanilla salt
- I teaspoon vanilla pepper

In a large bowl, combine parsley, scallions, mint, tomatoes, and toss gently.

In a small bowl, combine bulgur and water for 5 minutes, then drain.

In a separate bowl, combine olive oil, lemon juice, vanilla extract and caviar, vanilla salt and pepper, and mix. Add the bulgur to the oil mixture, and pour over the parsley mixture.

Enjoy it with a roasted Vanilla Leg of Lamb* and complement it with Vanilla Baba Ghanoush,* Vanilla Spanakopita,* or Vanilla Hummus.* Finish with Vanilla Baklava,* or go vegan without the lamb and enjoy everything else. So delicious!

*Recipes are in the index.

Protein: 3% 3kcal. Fat: 72% 86 kcal. Carbs: 25% 30 kcal

SOUPS

VANILLA POSOLE VERDE

VANILLA POSOLE VERDE

- I large onion, chopped
- 3 cloves garlic, minced
- I lb. pork, chunks
- 6 cups water
- 3 cans white hominy, drained and rinsed
- I tablespoon vanilla salt and pepper, to taste
- 2 cups roasted green chili (New Mexican), chopped
- 2 tablespoons vanilla caviar
- I tablespoon vanilla extract
- I tablespoon garlic powder
- I tablespoon onion powder
- I tablespoon red chili flake
- I tablespoon whole coriander, roasted
- I tablespoon whole cumin, roasted

Fresh lime squeeze and melted cheese on top

In a large pot, sauté onion and garlic, and cook on medium heat until translucent, for a few minutes. Add pork and brown lightly. Add water, scraping the browned goodies off the bottom with a wooden spoon. Add the coriander, cumin, hominy, garlic powder, onion powder, vanilla salt and pepper, cooking together for 30 minutes, until incorporated. Add green chili, vanilla extract and caviar, and let simmer for 10 minutes, then sprinkle on the red chili flakes. Enjoy with tortillas, flour or corn, and melt your favorite cheese on top. Yes!

Being a kid in New Mexico, I put chili verde (green chili) on everything and still do. This is a Christmas specialty, but I make it year-round. It's pure comfort in a bowl. Try it and I think you'll agree!

Protein: 35% 77 kcal. Fat: 44% 95 kcal. Carbs 21% 46 kcal

VANILLA PUMPKIN SOUP

VANILLA PUMPKIN SOUP

- I medium onion, chopped and browned
- I ½ lbs. of pumpkin, peeled and cubed
- 4 cups vegetable or chicken stock
- I large potato, peeled and cubed
- I clove garlic, minced
- I tablespoon olive oil
- I tablespoon vanilla caviar
- I tablespoon vanilla extract
- ¼ cup sour cream or plain yogurt
- Cognac for garnish

In a large pot, combine the onion and garlic in a little oil, and cook over low heat until translucent. Add the pumpkin, potato, and stock and bring to a boil. Reduce heat to simmer for 20 minutes or until the pumpkin is tender. Remove from heat and add vanilla caviar. Cool slightly and puree in a blender. Serve with a swirl of sour cream or yogurt and a drizzle of cognac with a few drops of vanilla extract mixed into it! Oh my goodness!

Another delightful dish from Australia and my dear friend Lorna Christian. Love you, Lorna!

Protein: 68% 560 kcal. Fat: 22% 186 kcal. Carbs: 10% 80 kcal

VANILLA LOBSTER BISQUE

- 2 cups chicken broth
- ½ lb. cooked lobster
- 1 cup dry white wine
- 1 ½ cup half and half, room temperature
- 3 tablespoons melted butter
- 4 teaspoons vanilla extract, divided
- ¼ cup chopped fresh mushrooms
- 2 tablespoons chopped onions
- 2 tablespoons chopped celery
- 2 tablespoons chopped carrot
- ¼ teaspoon vanilla salt and white pepper to taste
- ¼ teaspoon cayenne pepper
- 1 oz. vodka
- 1 teaspoon vanilla caviar
- 1 fresh lemon, juiced with zest

Melt butter and 2 teaspoons vanilla in a saucepan over medium-low heat. Add mushrooms, onion, celery, carrots, and cook until tender, about 10 minutes. Stir in chicken broth and season with vanilla salt, white pepper, and cayenne. Bring to a boil, then lower heat and simmer for 10 minutes. Set aside and let cool.

In a separate saucepan, sauté lobster for a minute and flambé with 1 oz. vodka and the remaining 2 teaspoons of vanilla extract. Set aside.

Pour slightly cooled vegetables mixture in a blender and add ¼ cup of lobster meat. Cover and process until smooth. Return to the saucepan and stir in half & half, wine, and rest of the lobster. Cook over low heat, stirring frequently until thickened. Fold in vanilla caviar, and finish with a squeeze of fresh lemon juice and zest. Serve with toasted baguette!

Protein: 66% 337 kcal. Fat: 28% 141 kcal. Carbs: 6% 32 kcal

SIDES

VANILLA POTATOES

VANILLA POTATOES

VANILLA ROASTED

- 3 lbs. small roasting potatoes, cleaned and cubed
- ¼ cup olive oil
- 1 tablespoon vanilla extract
- 1½ tablespoons vanilla caviar
- Vanilla salt and pepper to taste

Preheat the oven to 475 F degrees. Combine oil, extract, caviar, salt, and pepper, and mix well. Toss the potatoes in the mixture, coating evenly and thoroughly. Spread it on a baking sheet and roast for 20 to 30 minutes or until golden brown.

VANILLA HERB ROASTED

- Same recipe as above, adding to the mixture before tossing:
- 2 tablespoons minced fresh garlic
- ½ teaspoon each of dried basil, marjoram, dill, oregano, parsley, thyme, crushed red chili flakes

Combine these ingredients with the Vanilla Roasted recipe, and roast in the oven as above.

VANILLA MASHED POTATOES

- 6 Yukon potatoes, whole unpeeled
- 1 cup heavy cream
- 1 tablespoon vanilla extract
- 1 tablespoon vanilla caviar
- 1 tablespoon table salt
- Vanilla salt and pepper to taste
- 4 tablespoons butter, melted

Place potatoes in a saucepan big enough to hold them and cover with cold water. Add salt and bring to a boil, reduce heat, and simmer until the potatoes are tender when pierced with a fork, 15–25 minutes. Drain the potatoes and pass them through a potato ricer into a large bowl.

In a separate bowl, combine the cream, vanilla extract and caviar, and mix. Add this to the large bowl with the potatoes. Whip with a whisk or beater until it's creamy and smooth. Adjust the salt and pepper, and drizzle with melted vanilla butter. (Three tablespoons melted butter and ½ teaspoon vanilla extract.)

VANILLA POTATO PANCAKES/LATKES

- 2½–3 lbs. potatoes
- 2 onions, chopped
- 3 scallions, chopped
- 3 large eggs, lightly beaten
- 1 tablespoon vanilla caviar
- 1 teaspoon vanilla extract
- 1 teaspoon vanilla salt
- ½ teaspoon vanilla pepper
- ¼–¾ cup flour
- ½ cup canola oil + ¼ cup vanilla butter (½ teaspoon vanilla in ¼ cup butter) for frying
- Applesauce, vanilla sour cream, green onions, parsley for garnish

Coarsely grate potatoes and onion in a bowl, and squeeze the moisture out, removing as much liquid as possible.

In a separate bowl, mix together scallions, eggs, vanilla caviar and extract, vanilla salt, and pepper. Mix in the grated potatoes and onion, adding flour to bind them.

Heat a cast iron skillet, pour in the oil/butter mixture, covering the bottom and coming up the sides, about an eighth of an inch. Carefully drop a heaping tablespoon of the mixture, (wear an apron to reduce burns) into the hot oil, and flatten to form patties. Fry until golden on both sides and drain on paper towel. Garnish with parsley and serve with vanilla sour cream and applesauce.

Protein: 3% 21 kcal. Fat: 54% 324 kcal. Carbs: 43% 260 kcal

VANILLA CRISPY COCONUT RICE

- 4 cups cooked rice (cooked in equal parts water and coconut milk)
- 3 tablespoons coconut oil, divided
- 2 tablespoons peanut oil, divided
- 4 tablespoons toasted unsweetened coconut
- 1 tablespoon vanilla caviar
- 2 teaspoon vanilla extract
- 2 teaspoon vanilla salt
- 2 teaspoon vanilla white pepper
- 2 scallions chopped, for garnish

Heat a heavy skillet (big enough to hold the rice flattened) on medium heat with 2 tablespoons coconut oil and 1 tablespoon peanut oil.

In a bowl, mix cooked rice, toasted coconut, vanilla caviar, extract, salt, and pepper, gently turning it over and over until completely mixed.

Add the mixture to a hot oiled skillet and press into the pan (about ¾-inch thick), and sizzle it until it is golden brown. Turn over, adding remaining 1 tablespoon of coconut oil and 1 tablespoon of peanut oil, and cook on both sides until golden brown and crispy. Plate and cut into pieces, sprinkle with scallions, and serve with Vanilla Chicken Teriyaki*, eggs, fish, or on its own. Yummy!

This is a side dish that is served three times a day in Hawai'i. We gotta have our rice or poi!

*Recipe is in the index.

Protein: 6% 33 kcal. Fat: 23% 127 kcal. Carbs: 71% 399 kcal

VANILLA SPANAKOPITA

- 3 tablespoons olive oil, plus more for oiling pan and brushing
- 1 large onion, chopped
- 1 bunch scallions, chopped
- 2 cloves of garlic, minced
- 2 lbs. fresh spinach, rinsed and chopped
- ½ cup fresh parsley, chopped
- 1 cup crumbled feta cheese
- ½ cup ricotta cheese
- 2 large eggs, lightly beaten
- 3 teaspoon vanilla extract
- 1 tablespoon vanilla caviar
- Vanilla salt and pepper to taste
- 10 sheets of phyllo dough and ¼ cup olive oil, as needed

Preheat the oven to 350 F degrees, and lightly oil a 9-inch square baking pan.

In a large skillet, heat the olive oil at medium heat and sauté onions, scallions, and garlic in hot oil until soft and lightly browned, about 5 minutes. Add the vanilla caviar. Stir in spinach and parsley and continue to sauté until the spinach is limp, about 2 minutes. Remove from heat and cool.

In a bowl, combine the feta, ricotta, eggs, and vanilla extract, vanilla salt and pepper, and mix until well incorporated. Stir into the spinach mixture.

Lay one sheet of phyllo dough into the prepared baking pan, brushed lightly with olive oil. Lay down another sheet of phyllo and brush with oil, repeating this process five times. Spread spinach mixture evenly over top of the fifth layer of phyllo, folding overhanging dough over the filling. Continue to layer the rest of the phyllo dough, brushing each with oil and tucking the dough to seal in the filling.

Bake in a preheated oven until golden brown, 30 to 40 minutes. Cut into squares, and serve it hot or at room temperature. Pair this with Vanilla Hummus*, Vanilla Tabbouleh*, Vanilla Leg of Lamb*, or Vanilla Baba Ghanoush* for an amazing Mediterranean feast.

This feast always reminds me of my first bestie, Mary. Since the age of three years old, we played together every day, went to school together, and lived next door; we were inseparable. She's now a beautiful Greek woman, and oh my goodness the food at their house was out of this world and was nothing like my mom's home cooking! (Love you Mom!) Parties, church, and holidays, I was there.

My Mom had her own talents, she was the neighborhood hairdresser and had flare and panahe, with her saloon in our house. Everybody loved Peggie and her knack for making you look your best, by giving you the very latest styles! And I had them all and often got in trouble for creating my own hair styles on the neighborhood kids, while she was out for the evening! Ooops Peggie! She'd get so mad at me, then we'd laugh ourselves to tears. I know they're happily together now, they let me know often…

*Recipes are in the index.

Protein: 26% 30 kcal. Fat: 62% 72 kcal. Carbs: 12% 14 kcal

VANILLA GNOCCHI

- 1 8 to 12 ounces package of gnocchi
- 6 tablespoons butter
- 2 tablespoons vanilla extract
- Vanilla salt to taste
- Vanilla pepper to taste
- Pinch of nutmeg

Boil gnocchi in salted water until it's at a rolling boil with gnocchi on top.

In a separate saucepan, melt the butter, and brown it to a medium brown. Add the vanilla extract. Drain the gnocchi, and add it to the butter mixture. Cook for 5 minutes, adding in the vanilla salt, pepper, and nutmeg to taste.

This can be a flambé or add a fresh squeeze of lemon or lime, and serve as a bed with any kind of cooked seafood or fish.

This is the first simple recipe that I shared with the vanilla tour, to introduce folks to the savory application of vanilla!

Protein: 3% 8 kcal. Fat: 80% 244 kcal. Carbs: 17% 53 kcal

VANILLA SAFFRON DOLMADES

VANILLA SAFFRON DOLMADES

- 2 cups or 60 grape leaves, in jar with brine
- 1 cup medium rice, raw
- 1 cup of olive oil, divided
- 1 large onion, chopped
- 2 scallions, chopped
- 1½ tablespoons vanilla extract
- 6 threads of saffron
- 1 teaspoon vanilla caviar
- 1 bunch fresh dill, chopped
- 1 bunch parsley, chopped
- 6 mint leaves, chopped
- 2 fresh lemons, juiced
- Vanilla salt and pepper to taste

Remove the grape leaves, and rinse well in a strainer. Set aside to drain.

In a medium saucepan, sauté onions, saffron, and scallions for a few minutes on medium heat. Add mint, parsley, vanilla extract, and dill. Stir in rice, and add half of the olive oil and enough hot water to cover the rice. Bring to a boil. Boil 5 to 7 minutes, remove from heat, and cover with a clean tea towel for 10 minutes. Add the vanilla caviar, salt and pepper, and you're ready to start stuffing the grape leaves.

Open each leaf with the vein side up. One by one (if torn, set aside to line the bottom of the pan), place a teaspoon of mixture at the base of the leaf, fold in the sides, and roll in a tight roll. Go for tight and tidy rolls. Once all the leaves are rolled, place them on a layer of plain grape leaves (on the bottom) of a large pot, arranging them in a circular pattern, tightly together, not leaving any space between them. Then cover them with the remaining olive oil, lemon juice, and add just enough cold water to cover them. Add a heavy pot or a plate with a brick right on top of them. You must weigh them down or else they'll unravel while cooking. Cook on low to medium heat for 30 to 40 minutes. Remove from the pot and serve hot, or you can allow it to cool to room temperature and refrigerate. Hot or cold, these are one of my all-time favs!

*Recipes are in the index.

The combination of this, Vanilla Hummus*, Vanilla Baba ghanoush*, Vanilla Tabbouleh*, or Vanilla Leg of lamb* is an awesome combination. Spent a month and a half in Athens and had some of the best food I've tasted in the world. It is an amazing memory of walking about the plaka around the Acropolis, the open markets, the scent of the food, and the beautiful people. As I began my journey in childhood with my best friend Mary K., a sweet little Greek girl, it was befitting for me to travel there on assignment to critique the local fare for the magazine. I soaked it all in. I am surely blessed.

Protein: 1% 3 kcal. Fat: 90% 177 kcal. Carbs: 9% 17 kcal

VANILLA MAC 'N' CHEESE

VANILLA MAC 'N' CHEESE

- 1 lb. elbow macaroni (cooked al'dente)
- 4 tablespoons butter
- 4 tablespoons flour
- 2 teaspoons garlic powder
- 1 teaspoon dry mustard
- 1 teaspoon vanilla salt
- 2 teaspoons vanilla pepper
- Milk for roux
- 1 tablespoons vanilla extract
- 1 tablespoon vanilla caviar
- 1 lb. extra sharp cheddar cheese, grated (reserve ¼ cup)
- 1-8 oz. package Italian cheese mix
- 4 oz. prepared French-fried onions
- ¼ cup roasted macadamia nuts

Preheat the oven to 350 F degrees.

Cook macaroni according to box instructions, less 1–2 minutes, slightly al'dente, set aside.

Melt butter in a medium saucepan, and add the flour, garlic, mustard, salt, and pepper to make the roux. Sauté for about 3 to 5 minutes until the flour is cooked and slightly brown. If it's too thick, add a bit of milk to thin it out, but not too thin; you want it thickish. Add the vanilla extract, caviar, cheese mix, and the cheese (except reserved), and add the macaroni. Gently mix well, spread into a baking dish evenly, and top with the reserved cheese and French-fried onions. Bake for 30 minutes or until it is golden brown on top. Sprinkle with macadamia nuts and serve!

This one reminds me of dear friend Cathy, an awesome woman, and a pastor of a pretty little church in Hilo, Hawai'i. She is always so loving and gracious. She'd include me in Thanksgiving feasts, where she'd make this, and I couldn't get enough of it! Ironically, I was never a fan until her recipe. Yummy!

Protein: 14% 64 kcal. Fat: 46% 204 kcal. Carbs: 40% 177 kcal

VANILLA CREPES (SWEET AND SAVORY)

VANILLA CREPES (SWEET AND SAVORY)

- 1 egg per person served
- 2 tablespoons melted butter per person
- ¼ cup milk per person
- 2–3 tablespoons sifted flour per person (or more for consistency)
- Pinch of vanilla salt
- 1 teaspoon honey per person (for sweet) or ¼ teaspoon salt (for
- savory)
- ¼ teaspoon vanilla extract per person

Whisk eggs, butter, and milk together in a bowl. Add the sifted flour, stir well, then add a pinch of vanilla salt and vanilla extract. The batter should be loose and pour easily off the spoon. (If preparing savory, add more salt; if preparing sweet, add honey and less vanilla salt). Add more flour to achieve the proper consistency; it should be a light and runny pancake batter.

Heat oiled skillet or crepe pan to medium high heat, pour in 2–3 tablespoons of batter, moving the pan quickly in a circular motion to spread the batter evenly over the bottom. Cook until the crepe is bubbling, then flip it to the other side, approximately 2 minutes on each side. Stack each crepe on parchment paper, and cover with a clean cloth tea towel.

Fillings can be sweet or savory, from fruit to shrimp.

SWEET:
- Strawberries and whipped cream
- Peaches and cream
- Bananas foster
- Tropical island fruit blend with vanilla yogurt

SAVORY:
- Garlic shrimp
- Beef and sour cream
- Veggies and cheese
- Chicken and veggies

Protein: 30% 48 kcal. Fat: 61% 98 kcal. Carbs: 9% 15 kcal

VANILLA HUMMUS AND VANILLA BABA GHANOUSH

VANILLA HUMMUS

- 3 cups cooked chickpeas/garbanzo beans, peeled (1 ½ cup dried, cooked or quality canned)
- 2 cloves of garlic
- Ice cubes
- 1/3 cup tahini paste
- 1 tablespoon vanilla extract
- 1 teaspoon vanilla caviar
- 1 teaspoon vanilla salt
- ½ teaspoon ground cumin
- Juice and zest of a lemon
- Extra virgin olive oil
- Pita bread for serving

Add cooked garbanzo beans and garlic to a food processor and puree until a thick, powder-like mixture forms. While the processor is running, add an ice cube, tahini, vanilla extract and caviar, salt, cumin, and lemon juice and zest. Blend for about 4 minutes or until it's smooth. If the consistency is too thick, add some hot water a little at a time. Adjust the seasoning (I like a lot of lemon), and serve in a bowl with a drizzle of olive oil and some pita bread. Or make the complete Mediterranean feast!

Protein: 13% 33 kcal. Fat:46% 117 kcal. Carbs: 41% 104 kcal

VANILLA BABA GHANOUSH

- 1 large eggplant, sliced
- 2 tablespoons tahini paste
- 1 lemon, juiced with zest
- 2 cloves garlic
- 1 teaspoon vanilla salt and pepper
- 1 tablespoon Greek yogurt
- 1 teaspoon vanilla caviar
- 1 teaspoon vanilla extract
- 1 teaspoon ground cumin
- ½ teaspoon smoked paprika
- Extra virgin olive oil for drizzling
- Parsley for garnish
- Pita bread for serving

Preheat the oven to 400 F degrees.

Spread a thin layer of oil on each side of the sliced eggplant, and roast the eggplant in the oven or on the grill for 20 minutes, or until it is completely cooked through. On the grill (preferred), cook until it is slightly charred. Let cool.

In a large bowl, combine the remaining ingredients. Once the eggplant is cooled, remove the skin, and add these slices in with the rest of the combined ingredients. Mash until it is all combined well. Serve with a drizzle of olive oil and top with fresh parsley, along with pita bread.

Protein: 10% 9 kcal. Fat: 45% 38 kcal. Carbs: 45% 38 kcal

ENTREES

VANILLA BROWN BUTTER SHRIMP

VANILLA BROWN BUTTER SHRIMP

- 1 lb. shrimp
- 6 tablespoons butter
- 1 tablespoon garlic, minced
- 4 teaspoons vanilla extract, divided

⅛ cup vodka

- ½ teaspoon vanilla salt and pepper to taste
- Fresh lemon or lime juice and zest
- Chives for garnish

Boil or sauté shrimp for 2 to 4 minutes, then set aside.

In a skillet, sauté the butter gently until it is slightly browned, add garlic. Add 2 teaspoons vanilla extract, and cook low and slow for 2 minutes.

Heat the pan that the shrimp are in and quickly flambe the shrimp for 1 minute in a mixture of the vodka with 2 teaspoons vanilla. Add this to the browned butter mixture, and add vanilla salt and pepper. Put a squeeze of fresh citrus or passion fruit over the top, garnish with chives, and serve on rice or riced cauliflower and a Vanilla Salad Niçoise.*

*Recipe is in the index.

Protein: 36% 92 kcal. Fat 62% 157 kcal. Carbs: 2% 4 kcal

VANILLA BLACK AND BLUE AHI

VANILLA BLACK AND BLUE AHI

- 1 lb. fresh Ahi, cut into steaks
- 2 tablespoons of each vanilla salt, pepper, and sugar
- 1 teaspoon vanilla caviar
- 2 tablespoons butter
- 2 tablespoons olive oil
- 2 teaspoons vanilla extract

Freeze the fresh steaks for 5 minutes.

Mix salt, pepper, sugar, and caviar together in a bowl and set aside.

In a skillet, heat the oil and butter together until it begins to smoke. Coat the 1 ½ inch steaks with vanilla extract, thoroughly coat them in the salt, pepper, and sugar mixture, and gently put them in the hot smoking pan. Sear the steaks for 60 to 90 seconds per side.

Serve with Vanilla Aioli for Fish and Fowl* atop a bed of greens and a side of Vanilla Coconut Rice.*

Ono-Licious, or should I say, Ahi-Licious!

*These recipes are in the index.

Protein: 57% 118 kcal. Fat: 43% 90 kcal. Carbs: 0% 1 kcal

VANILLA STEAK KIANE (DIANE)

VANILLA STEAK KIANE (DIANE)

- 1 lb. beef tenderloin, cut into 1 ½ inch steaks
- 2 tablespoons whole white pepper, cracked
- 2 teaspoon vanilla salt
- 2 tablespoons butter
- 2 tablespoons olive oil
- ½ cup brandy cognac with 2 teaspoons vanilla extract
- 1 cup heavy whipping cream, room temperature
- 1 tablespoon vanilla caviar

Season steaks on both sides with cracked pepper and salt. Heat butter and oil in a large cast iron skillet over medium-high heat. Brown steaks on both sides, about 3–5 minutes. Transfer steaks to a plate with a tin foil tent.

Remove skillet from the heat and drain drippings. Pour in a little more than half the brandy (with the extract), and flambe carefully with a long match, shaking the skillet back and forth until the flames die down, about 30 seconds. Return the skillet to medium heat, whisk in cream, and simmer. Cook until the sauce coats the back of a spoon, 5–6 minutes, whisking occasionally and watching it. Stir in the rest of the brandy/vanilla mixture plus the vanilla caviar, and return the steaks to skillet and heat through, 1–2 minutes. Serve with roasted Brussels sprouts, Vanilla Potatoes,* and a good red wine.

*Recipe is in the index.

Protein: 33% 152 kcal. Fat 65% 301 kcal. Carbs: 2% 11 kcal

VANILLA CHICKEN TANDOORI

VANILLA CHICKEN TANDOORI

TANDOORI SPICE (DRY) MIX
- I teaspoon ground cumin
- I teaspoon ground coriander
- I teaspoon ground ginger
- I teaspoon ground paprika
- I teaspoon ground turmeric
- I teaspoon vanilla salt
- I teaspoon vanilla caviar
- I teaspoon vanilla pepper
- I teaspoon cayenne pepper

CHICKEN
- I whole chicken
- I lemon, juice
- I cup plain yogurt
- I ½ tablespoons vanilla extract

Preheat the oven to 450 F degrees.

In a bowl, whisk together the tandoori spices and set aside.

Take the whole chicken and loosen the skin from the flesh, gently to not rip the skin, and rub the outside of the chicken with lemon.

Combine in a bowl the spice mix with yogurt, vanilla extract, and mix until completely incorporated. Take the mixture and with your hand slide it in between the skin and the flesh of the chicken. Place into a casserole pan.

Place the chicken in the oven for 15 minutes, then reduce the heat to 400 F degrees and cook for another 30–50 minutes, or until it's golden brown and the juices run clear. Remove the chicken from the oven and allow it to rest for 15 minutes.

Cut and serve with basmati rice and roasted veggies.

This is one you must try, as it hits all the taste sensors and spreads joy throughout your body!

Protein: 71% 216 kcal. Fat: 25% 76 kcal. Carbs: 4% 13 kcal

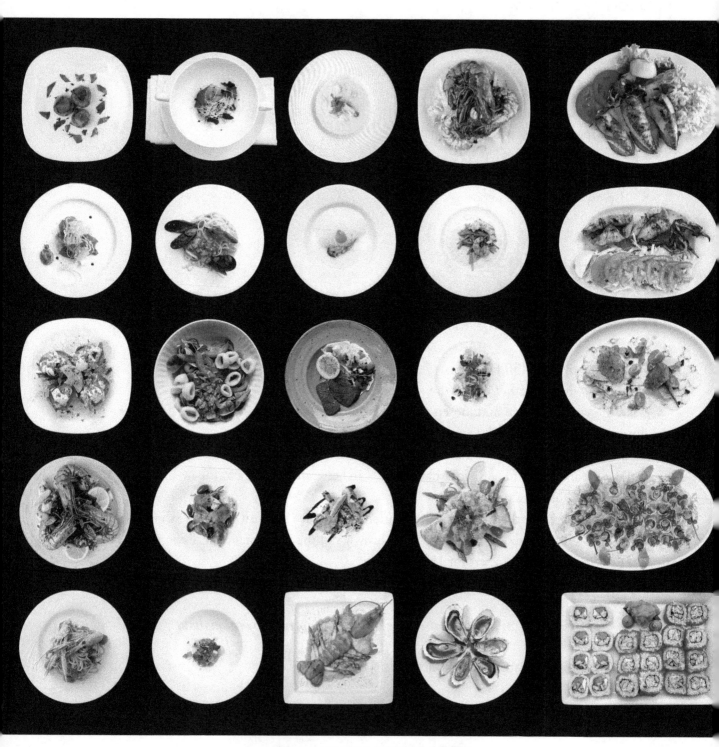

VANILLA AIOLI FOR FISH AND FOWL

VANILLA AIOLI FOR FISH AND FOWL

The following recipes start with a store-bought rotisserie chicken; you know the one! And with fish of all varieties. All of these recipes can be served warm or cold, with whole or chopped fish or chicken. Best to have them all on hand!

VANILLA CURRY AIOLI
- ½ cup mayonnaise
- ½ cup plain yogurt
- 3 tablespoons curry powder
- 2 tablespoons whole coriander seeds
- 1 tablespoon whole white pepper
- 1 teaspoon ground ginger
- 2 teaspoons garlic powder
- ½ teaspoon vanilla caviar
- 1 teaspoon vanilla extract
- Vanilla salt and pepper to taste
- 1 tablespoon wine vinegar

Mix all of the ingredients in a bowl, and let it set up for an hour. Serve it over hot or cold chicken, whole or diced chicken. Serve it with chutney, fruits, raisins, banana, yogurt, rice, or salad.

VANILLA CHIPOTLE GREEN CHILI AIOLI
- 1 cup mayonnaise
- ¼ cup smashed prepared canned chipotle (or less)
- ¼ cup diced green chili
- 1 teaspoon ground cumin
- 1 tablespoon whole coriander
- 1 tablespoon whole white pepper
- ¼ cup chopped onion
- 2 cloves fresh garlic, minced
- 1 tablespoon vanilla caviar
- 1 teaspoon vanilla extract
- 1 lime, juiced with zest
- ¼ cup chopped chives (or cilantro or both)

Mix all the ingredients together in a bowl, and allow it to sit for a 1 hour or longer. Serve over chicken, with tortillas, black beans, and Vanilla Guacamole.*

*The recipe is in the index.

VANILLA LEMON AIOLI FOR SEAFOOD OR CHICKEN

- 1 cup mayonnaise
- ¼ chopped red onion
- ¼ cup chopped celery
- 1 tablespoon dried dill
- 1 teaspoon garlic powder
- 3 tablespoons chopped sweet pickle relish
- 1 teaspoon vanilla extract
- 1 teaspoon vanilla caviar
- 1 lemon, juiced and zest

Mix all the ingredients together in a bowl, and allow it to marry for at least 1 hour. Serve over seafood or chicken. Delicious!

Protein: 7% 10 kcal. Fat: 83% 115 kcal. Carbs: 9% 13 kcal

I drove my sweet Mom crazy with my strange childhood diet of mayonnaise and lettuce sandwiches along with celery soup. Love my mayo! It's all I would eat for the longest time, talk about boring. Little did I know beyond that, there were amazing menus and recipes from around the world, paved in mayo! I have to admit, my first Macdonald's was pretty much my last, almost hurled. Oh yuck. I'll stick to my mayo sandwiches, thank you very much, and when I found out about aioli, oh my goodness! It's heavenly. Love it!

VANILLA CHICKEN TERIYAKI

- I cup sugar
- I cup shoyu (soy sauce)
- 4 tablespoons minced fresh garlic
- 4 tablespoons minced fresh ginger
- 3 tablespoons vanilla extract
- I tablespoon vanilla caviar
- 6 chicken thighs, cleaned and dried
- 6 edible flowers for garnish (optional)
- Chopped scallions and cilantro for garnish

In a small bowl, mix the sugar and shoyu together and allow it to sit at room temperature for 1 hour. Add the minced garlic, ginger, and vanilla extract and caviar, mix well. Submerge the chicken into the mix and marinate overnight in the refrigerator.

Cooking on the grill is preferable, but it can be roasted in a 400 F degree oven for 20 to 30 minutes, basting it either way. Serve over Vanilla Crispy Coconut Rice,* and garnish with scallions, cilantro, and an orchid. Aloha.

If you've been to Hawai'i, you know dis da bes! It's served everywhere and is an island delight for sure!

Recipe is in the index.

Protein: 27% 137 kcal. Fat: 57% 290 kcal. Carbs: 16% 80 kcal

VANILLA LINGUINE AND CLAMS

VANILLA LINGUINE AND CLAMS

- 1 lb. linguine pasta
- 3 dozen fresh medium clams or 4 cans of minced clams
- ½ cup extra virgin olive oil
- 4 cloves of garlic, peeled and minced
- 1½ tablespoons vanilla extract
- 1 tablespoon flour
- 1 Fresh lemon juice and 1 teaspoon of zest
- 1 teaspoon vanilla caviar
- Vanilla salt and pepper to taste
- Red chili flakes for garnish
- Chives or parsley for garnish

If you're using fresh clams, rinse them out in a bowl of water and then add 1 tablespoon of corn-meal and let them soak for 10 minutes. Scrub each one under water to remove all the sand, drain and chill. If you're using canned, just open it! Drain the juice and reserve it.

Meanwhile, bring a large pot of water to boil, generously salted. When ready add the linguine and cook until tender, but al'dente; do not overcook it. Read the package, and do 2 minutes less.

In a skillet on the side, heat olive oil, add garlic and cook until translucent, then add the vanilla extract. Stir in the flour and cook it off for about 5 minutes (taste it), creating a roux. Add the reserved clam juice or stock from fresh clams, lemon juice and zest, vanilla caviar, vanilla salt, and pepper. If it's too thick, thin with room temperature milk. If it's too thin, add more roux. Roux is your friend! Add the clams last, and mix it gently. Plate the pasta and top clam sauce with fresh parsley or chives and red chili flakes. Buon Appetito. Viva la Italia!

Protein: 6% 11 kcal. Fat: 73% 80 kcal. Carbs: 90% 179 kcal

VANILLA ROASTED LAMB

VANILLA ROASTED LAMB

- 4-5 lbs boneless leg of lamb or rack of lamb
- 4 cloves of garlic, minced
- 2 tablespoons Dijon mustard
- Springs of fresh rosemary
- 3 tablespoons vanilla extract
- ¼ cup dried vanilla powder
- 5 lemons, juiced
- ¼ cup olive oil
- 2 tablespoons Herbs de Provence
- 1 tablespoon vanilla salt and pepper

Preheat the oven to 450 F degrees.

Untie the leg of lamb (if it's tied), and open it up, trimming off the fatter pieces of fat.

In a small bowl, whisk together garlic, vanilla extract, lemon, mustard, herbs de Provence, vanilla salt, pepper, and olive oil. Set aside.

Dry rub the leg of lamb with the vanilla powder and allow it to sit for an hour. Then spread the garlic oil mixture all over the lamb, and pierce the lamb with the sprigs of fresh rosemary.

Roast in the oven for 15 minutes, then reduce the heat to 350 F degrees for 1 to 1½ hours or until the internal temperature registers 135 degrees. Remove the roast from the oven, and allow it to rest for 20 to 30 minutes before carving.

Serve with Mediterranean sides (recipes included) and roasted potatoes.

Protein: 36% 196 kcal. Fat: 64% 11 kcal. Carbs: 0% 0 kcal

VANILLA CHICKEN KIEV

VANILLA CHICKEN KIEV

- 4 boneless chicken breasts, sprinkled lightly with vanilla salt and
- pepper, pounded out to a ½ inch thick
- 12 tablespoons butter
- 1 ½ cup panko breadcrumb
- 2 eggs, beaten with 1 teaspoon vanilla extract
- 2 cloves garlic, crushed
- ¼ teaspoon vanilla salt
- ½ teaspoon vanilla pepper
- 2 tablespoons chopped mix of parsley, oregano, tarragon, chives
- 1 tablespoon vanilla caviar, divided
- ½ cup flour

Vegetable oil to fry

Preheat the oven to 400 F degrees.

Combine garlic, salt, and pepper and mash together, adding the Italian herb mix and mash it all together until it's all mixed well. Add butter and vanilla caviar, mix well. Place the butter combination in a piece of plastic wrap, roll it up, and refrigerate it for a half hour to 1 hour or until it's solid.

Meanwhile, prepare your chicken breasts by placing them between two sheets of plastic wrap and pounding them with a rolling pin until even and flat, to about ¼- to ½-inch thick. Remove the prepared butter from the refrigerator and roll a piece of it up into the inside of the chicken breasts by tucking the ends of the chicken inward around the butter, completely encasing the butter into the chicken, laying them seam side down on a plate.

Heat oil in a saucepan on medium-high heat, and get out a baking sheet. Meanwhile, carefully brush the chicken with ½ tablespoon caviar and beaten egg and vanilla extract mixture all over it, and roll it in the breadcrumbs and flour. Place the chicken seam side down into a saucepan with hot oil, frying it gently on both sides for 1 minute and removing it to the baking sheet, seam side down, blotting some of the excess oil off. Sprinkle the chicken with salt and pepper and bake for 20 minutes or until it's golden brown.

Serve with a side of Vanilla Potatoes* and a salad. Scrumptious combination!

*Recipe is in the index.

Protein:25% 204 kcal. Fat: 58% 464 kcal. Carbs:5% 75 kcal

VANILLA GRUYERE SOUFFLE

- 1 cup whole milk, hot
- 5 large egg whites, room temperature
- 4 large egg yolks, room temperature
- 2½ tablespoons butter, room temperature
- 2–3 tablespoons all-purpose flour
- 2 tablespoons parmesan cheese, grated
- 1 cup shredded gruyere cheese (reserve 2 tablespoons)
- 1 tablespoon vanilla extract
- 1½ teaspoons vanilla caviar
- ½ teaspoon vanilla salt
- ½ teaspoon vanilla white pepper
- ¼ teaspoon cream tartar
- Pinch of nutmeg

Preheat the oven to 400 F degrees. Prepare 8-ounce ramekins or medium souffle (adding parchment paper collar on pan, not ramekins) by buttering and dusting with parmesan cheese, thoroughly covering bottom and sides.

Melt the butter in a saucepan over medium-high heat, and whisk in the flour, making a roux. Cook it until it starts to brown and add vanilla extract. Whisk in the hot milk until the mixture thickens, about 2–3 minutes. Remove from the heat, and whisk in the nutmeg, vanilla salt, and white pepper. Slowly begin to whisk in the egg yolks one at a time, add the vanilla caviar, and once incorporated transfer it to a bowl and cover with plastic wrap to keep from forming a skin. Let this batter cool to room temperature.

In a separate metal bowl (the French love to do it in copper), beat the egg whites with an electric mixer until frothy. Add the cream of tartar and continue to beat to stiff peaks, not dry. Gently fold in one large spoonful of batter, then gently fold in the gruyere cheese together with egg whites, alternating until all is gently folded together.

Put the mixture into the prepared pans and place them in a water bath (bain-marie, two inches of water in the bottom of a baking pan) on the bottom rack of the oven, baking for 20 minutes, in a quiet undisturbed kitchen. Bake until it's golden brown and sprinkle the reserved cheese for the last 5 minutes until the souffle has set and the cheese is melted. Enjoy this as a main course with a Vanilla Salad Niçoise* or as a side to grilled chicken or fish. Souffle's are not hard to do; just be prepared, patient, and quiet. Bon appetit!

We loved traveling through the alps of Switzerland tasting along the way, the absolute best cheese on the planet; gruyere was our favorite. Michael loved his grilled cheese sandwiches made with this cheese and sometimes with no bread, just grilled cheese and fruit! Try gruyere and dark chocolate together!

*Recipe is in the index.

Protein: 30% 81 kcal. Fat: 56% 152 kcal. Carbs: 14% 37 kcal

DESSERTS

("stressed" spelled backward)

VANILLA MACADAMIA CREPE CAKE

VANILLA MACADAMIA CREPE CAKE

CREPES
- 6 eggs room temperature
- I cup milk, room temperature
- ¾ cup butter, room temperature
- I tablespoons vanilla caviar
- I tablespoon extract
- Pinch vanilla salt
- 3 tablespoons vanilla sugar
- I/2–¾ cup all-purpose whole wheat white flour, sifted
- ½ cup roasted chopped Hawai'ian macadamia nuts
- Parchment paper for layering the crepes

FILLING
- 8 oz. cream cheese, softened
- ¾ cup butter, softened
- I/3 cup vanilla sugar (finely pulsed in blender)
- 2 tablespoons vanilla caviar
- I tablespoon vanilla extract
- Pinch of fresh ground nutmeg
- Pinch zest of lemon

For the crepe batter: Hand whisk the eggs and add the milk, butter, vanilla extract and caviar, vanilla salt, and vanilla sugar, until gently blended. Add in sifted flour gradually until it becomes a thin pancake consistency that runs smoothly off the whisk. Cover.

For the filling: In a separate bowl, combine the softened cream cheese, butter, ground vanilla sugar, vanilla caviar and extract, nutmeg, and lemon, gently folding and setting aside in a cool covered place.

MAKING THE CREPES

Heat enough oil to cover a 6- to 10-inch sauté or crepe pan or skillet. Pour about 2-3 tablespoons of the prepared batter in the pan while swirling it around the pan to cover the bottom lightly. If there is too much batter, pour it off. You should be able to almost see through it. When it begins to bubble, flip it over to brown it slightly, stacking them on a clean dish towel lined with parchment paper. Repeat until the batter is gone.

Lay the first crepe on the serving platter, smear on a bit of the filling, top with another crepe, and continue with a sprinkle of the macadamia nuts every 3rd or 4th crepe, reserving some nuts for the top. When you've completed stacked the cake, top it with edible flowers. Beautiful and tasty!

Protein: II% 58 kcal. Fat: 72% 368 kcal. Carbs: I6% 83 kcal

VANILLA MACADAMIA SHORTBREAD

VANILLA MACADAMIA SHORTBREAD

- 1 cup softened butter
- 1 cup powdered sugar
- 2 cup all-purpose flour
- 1½ tablespoons vanilla extract
- 1 teaspoon vanilla caviar
- ½ cup finely ground macadamia nuts
- ½ teaspoon vanilla salt
- 1 egg white with 1 tablespoon water (for egg wash)
- Course vanilla sugar, for sprinkling
- Juice and zest of 1 lemon, lime, or juice of lilikoi (passionfruit)

Preheat the oven to 325 F degrees, and line a baking sheet with parchment paper.

In a bowl using a hand mixer, beat the butter and powdered sugar, adding the vanilla extract, caviar, zest and lemon juice. Add the flour, macadamia nuts, and salt until combined, and you can press the dough together into a cohesive ball with your hands. Wrap it in plastic wrap and refrigerate for 30 minutes.

On a floured surface, roll out the dough into an 8x8 square about ½-inch thick. Cut the dough into 2-inch squares and place them on the prepared baking pan. Brush with egg white/water wash, and sprinkle them with coarse vanilla sugar. Bake for 18-20 minutes until golden brown.

Protein: 4% 12 kcal. Fat: 64% 207 kcal. Carbs: 32% 104 kcal

VANILLA CRÈME BRULEE

VANILLA CRÈME BRULEE

- 4 cups heavy cream
- 7 egg yolks
- ¾ cup vanilla sugar for creme
- 1 whole vanilla pod, scored lengthwise
- ¼ teaspoon vanilla salt
- ¾ cup vanilla sugar for top to brulee

Prepare a bain-marie, a water bath, by heating the oven to 300 F degrees and placing a roasting pan in it with 1 inch of water on the bottom.

In a saucepan, gently heat the cream on medium heat along with half the sugar (¼ cup + 2 tablespoons). Place the scored vanilla pod, scraping out some of the vanilla caviar into the saucepan, and heat over medium until the mixture thickens and starts to bubble, about 7 to 8 minutes. Do not let it boil. Stay with it and watch it.

Meanwhile, whisk egg yolks together in a large bowl with the remaining sugar and vanilla salt.

Temper the mixture by ladling a small amount of the hot cream into the egg mixture, whisking to combine, adding a small amount of hot cream to the eggs until it's completely together and combined. Strain the mixture through a mesh sieve into a bowl, removing the vanilla pod. Divide the custard into a ramekin or into a baking dish and place the pan into the prepared water bath. Bake for 30 to 40 minutes or until the custard has set. Remove it from the oven and water bath, allowing it to cool on a wire rack for 30 minutes. Cover it with plastic, and chill in the refrigerator for 2 hours.

To caramelize (burlee) the top, sprinkle 1½ teaspoons of the ¾ cup of vanilla sugar on top and pass a flame torch about 2 inches above in a circular motion, until the sugar bubbles and browns, forming a smooth surface. Serve immediately!

This is one of my son's all-time favorites! We were fortunate to spend many summers together in Provence, France, where we were totally spoiled by chefs wanting great reviews. We enjoyed some of the best food on the globe. At the time, he was a fluent French speaker and tutor at Punahou Schools (smart kiddo, received a full private scholarship!) where they had to declare a second language early in their education. His choice was the language of diplomats, which he was from the day he was born. He was a pure diplomat of Aloha. He was as beautiful on the inside as he was on the outside, sweet and gentle, everyone that knew Michael, loved Michael.

Protein: 5% 16 kcal. Fat: 79% 231 kcal. Carbs: 15% 45 kcal

VANILLA BEAN ICE CREAM

- 3 cups half & half
- 3 cups heavy cream
- 2 cups sugar
- 8 egg yolks
- 2 tablespoons vanilla extract
- 1 tablespoon vanilla caviar (scored from the pod, reserve pod)
- Pinch vanilla salt
- Ice cream machine

Heat the half & half and sugar in a saucepan over low heat. Add the vanilla caviar, extract and the vanilla pod, making sure to remove the pod later.

In a separate bowl, beat the egg yolks by hand until they are a pale yellow in color and thicker, add salt. Temper the egg yolks by drizzling a 1½ cups of the hot half & half. Mix it in slowly, whisking constantly.

Put that mixture together into a pan over medium heat and cook until quite thick, stirring constantly.

Drain the custard through a fine mesh or cheese cloth, (remove pod) and combine in a bowl with the heavy cream, stirring to blend. Chill the mixture thoroughly, and then freeze it in the ice cream maker, according to the manufacturer's instructions.

Serve it with something different other than chocolate alongside it, though they love each other deeply, chocolate and vanilla were found together by the Western world in Mexico initially. It's nice to try something different too! I love it with fresh fruit, a drizzle of caramel, or a drizzle of vanilla extract, a drizzle of cognac or bourbon, or a nice dark chocolate. Or try what I've introduced to many visitors from around the world at The Vanillerie. A whole new way to enjoy vanilla ice cream is with fresh ground white vanilla pepper on top. Oh my, yummy yummy! And while we're at it, try chocolate with a completely different twist: a side of brie, camembert, or even Rochefort cheese. What a delightful surprise!

Protein: 3% 4 kcal. Fat: 50% 75 kcal. Carbs: 48% 72 kcal

VANILLA MACADAMIA FUDGE

- 2 cups of vanilla sugar
- 2/3 cup of evaporated milk
- 1/3 cup milk
- 1/8 teaspoon vanilla salt
- ¼ cup butter
- 2 teaspoons vanilla extract
- 1 teaspoon vanilla caviar
- ½ cup roasted macadamia nuts, chopped

Butter an 8-inch square baking dish.

Butter the sides of a 2-quart heavy saucepan, then add in both milks, sugar, and salt. Cook over medium heat, stirring until it boils. Attach a candy thermometer to the side and continue to cook over medium-low heat until it reaches 238 F degrees or at the soft ball stage. Remove from heat and add butter, vanilla extract and vanilla caviar. Stop stirring! Allow it to cool to 110 F degrees and remove the thermometer. Beat with a wooden spoon until the fudge is thick and begins to lose its gloss. Fold in nuts and pour it into the prepared buttered dish. Cool and score the fudge into squares. Store in an airtight container.

I like it with a sprinkle of Hawai'ian vanilla salt on top! YUM!

Protein: 3% 4 kcal. Fat: 50% 75 kcal. Carbs: 48% 58 kcal

VANILLA CHEESECAKE

VANILLA CHEESECAKE

- 24 oz. cream cheese, room temp
- 4 eggs, room temperature
- ¾ cup sugar (super fine)
- 2 teaspoons vanilla extract
- 2 teaspoons vanilla caviar
- ¾ sour cream, room temperature
- 1 teaspoon lemon zest
- Pinch of Hawai'ian vanilla salt
- Fruit, pineapple, strawberries, passion fruit, etc. for topping

Preheat oven to 325 F degrees

Wrap the outside of a 9-inch springform pan with heavy aluminum foil to make it waterproof, oiling the interior of the pan with butter or coconut oil.

In a stand-up mixer, beat the cream cheese, add the sugar, vanilla extract, and caviar, mix well. Add sour cream and scrap the sides of the bowl down, as needed, mixing thoroughly. Gently add the eggs one at a time, mixing very gently to not overmix. Add the remaining ingredients (except fruit), and blend until smooth.

Pour the cheesecake batter into a prepared springform pan, and place that pan in a bain-marie (water bath half filled with water in a roasting pan).

Bake for 70 to 90 minutes until set and golden brown on top. The top shouldn't jiggle too much when set. Turn off the oven and open the oven door slightly. Leave it for 30 minutes. Remove the cake from the oven and place it on the counter. Allow it to cool to room temperature. Remove the sides of the springform, and continue to cool in the refrigerator until completely set, several hours.

Serve it as is, or top it with your favorite fruit. Mine is passion fruit. Share and enjoy!

Protein: 12% 47 kcal. Fat: 78% 283 kcal. Carbs: 15% 58 kcal

VANILLA PAVLOVA

VANILLA PAVLOVA

- 4 large eggs, separated at room temp
- 1 cup castor sugar (superfine)
- Pinch of vanilla salt
- ½ tablespoon cornstarch
- 2 teaspoon vanilla caviar
- 1 teaspoon vanilla extract
- 1 teaspoon vinegar

FRUIT ON TOP

- 2 cups of passion fruit(preferably) or whole berries, kiwi, etc.
- Sprig of fresh mint, optional

WHIPPED CREAM

- 1 cup heavy cream
- 1 teaspoon vanilla extract
- 2 tablespoons confectioner's sugar (see below)

Heat oven to 300 F degrees with the rack in the middle position.

On parchment paper, using a bowl as a guide, trace an 8-inch circle on the paper with a pencil, line a baking sheet with it, pencil side down, set aside.

In a clean medium-sized bowl, beat the egg whites with an electric mixer on medium speed until the whites start to form soft peaks. Gently sprinkle 1 tablespoon of sugar at a time into the egg whites, beating continuously until the whites are stiff with glossy peaks. Sprinkle the cornstarch on top and a pinch of salt. On the side, mix together vanilla caviar and extract into the vinegar and gently fold it all together with a spatula. Gently spread the meringue in the circle on the parchment paper, making a circular ring base, making sure the edges are slightly higher than the center, so that you can fill the well in the middle full of fruit after it's baked.

Place the baking sheet in the oven and reduce heat to 250 F degrees. Bake for 1 hour and 15 minutes or until it turns a pale eggshell color.

Turn off the oven, and leave the door ajar, allowing it to cool completely. It will crack slightly. Once cooled, place desired fruit in the center and top with whipped cream.

FOR THE WHIPPED CREAM:

Whip the heavy cream in a clean chilled deep bowl by beating with a whisk or hand mixer until soft peaks form. Sprinkle in the vanilla extract and confectioner's sugar (powdered sugar), and beat to return to soft peaks. Beat a bit more to stiff peaks, but don't over beat or it'll turn to butter! Refrigerate covered until serving.

Use the egg yolks for a custard or hollandaise.

An Australian delight!

Protein: 12% 29 kcal. Fat: 33% 78 kcal. Carbs: 55% 131 kcal

VANILLA SOUFFLE

VANILLA SOUFFLE

- 1 ⅓ cups whole milk, warmed and divided
- 4 large eggs, separated
- ⅓ cup of all-purpose flour
- ½ vanilla pod
- 7 tablespoons vanilla sugar (pulsed in blender to fine consistency)
- 1½ tablespoons unsalted butter and sugar for dish
- 1½ teaspoons vanilla extract
- 1 teaspoon vanilla caviar
- Pinch vanilla salt
- A bit of lemon zest
- ¼ teaspoon cream tartar
- ½ cup confectioner's sugar
- Fresh fruit, berries, banana, pineapple, mango, etc.

Preheat the oven to 350 F degrees. Prepare a large soufflé pan (adding collar to pan) by buttering the bottom and sides thoroughly, and then dust with sugar to cover the butter.

Heat 1 cup of milk with the scored vanilla pod to a steam, over low heat in a pan, set aside.

In a bowl whisk together 5 tablespoons of vanilla sugar and 2 egg yolks, blend, and add the flour and remaining milk. Mix until it forms a smooth batter. Slowly whisk in the hot milk (remove and reserve pod) into the batter, making sure all ingredients are combined. This is tempering. Add the tempered batter back to the milk and simmer, stirring constantly, until it's thickened, about a minute or two. Stir the melted butter into the mixture, and allow it to cool to room temperature. Add the vanilla extract, caviar, and lemon zest.

In a copper or metal mixing bowl with an electric mixer, beat the egg whites until frothy and add the cream of tartar and the remaining 2 tablespoons of vanilla sugar, then continue to beat until stiff but not dry. Fold in one large spoonful into the batter. Then very gently fold in the remaining egg whites, allowing some very small lumps.

Bake for 30 minutes in a bain-marie. It's a water bath made by placing ramekins in a cake pan and filling the pan with hot water to about an inch or two. Be quiet and do not open the oven during that time. Bake until golden brown (baking for up to an additional 5 minutes if needed).

Dust with confectioner's sugar, and top with fruit and an edible flower.

Protein: 30% 81 kcal. Fat: 56% 152 kcal. Carbs: 14% 37 kcal

VANILLA AVO MACADAMIA PIE

CRUST

- 1½ cups ground roasted macadamia nuts + reserve for garnish
- 2½ tablespoons butter, softened
- 1 teaspoon vanilla caviar
- 2 tablespoons brown sugar

FILLING

- 3 cups of mashed avocado with lemon
- ½ can sweetened condensed milk
- 2 teaspoons vanilla extract
- Pinch of Hawai'ian vanilla salt
- Juice and zest of 3 lemons or limes
- Whipped cream for garnish

Make the crust first to allow for cooling. In a medium bowl, mix together nuts, butter, vanilla caviar, and sugar. Press it into a 9-inch pie plate. Bake at 325 F degrees for 10 minutes or until the edge is golden brown. Set aside to fully cool.

Once the crust is cooled, make the filling. In a blender, add the avocado, milk, vanilla extract, vanilla salt, and lemon or lime juice and zest, pureeing together in a blender. Pour the filling into the cooled crust and chill in the refrigerator, covered for at least for 2 hours. Serve with fresh whipped cream. Delicious! You can always use the egg yolks to make custard or hollandaise.

This came from Gran's yard on Norfolk Island. She had macadamia, lemon, and avocado trees, and we all had a blast coming up with this one! Oh how Michelangelo and I loved being in her kitchen! They loved each other so very much.

Protein: 4% 16 kcal. Fat: 85% 378 kcal. Carbs: 11% 50 kcal

VANILLA BAKLAVA

- 1 1/4 lb. coarsely ground walnuts
- 1 lb. coarsely ground almonds
- 2 tablespoons ground cinnamon
- 3 tablespoons vanilla caviar
- 1 lb. phyllo dough
- 1 lb. melted butter

HONEY SYRUP
- 3½ cups sugar
- 2 cups water
- 1 cup honey
- 1 stick cinnamon
- 3 teaspoons vanilla extract
- 1/2 teaspoon vanilla salt
- 3 tablespoons fresh lemon juice

Get out a 10 1/2 x 15 x 2-inch ungreased baking pan.

In a large bowl, mix nuts, ground cinnamon, and vanilla caviar. Brush the baking pan with butter on all sides. Place the first layer of phyllo dough on the bottom of the pan and continue to layer each one with butter for seven sheets (setting aside 6–8 phyllo dough sheets for the top). On top the 7th layer of phyllo sprinkle evenly the nut mixture and continue layering alternating with the nut mixture and phyllo until all the nuts are used up. Add the 6–8 reserved layers of phyllo dough, buttering each one except for the top layer.

With a sharp serrated knife, cut the baklava into vertical strips 1-inch wide, making sure to cut to the bottom. Then cut strips diagonally 1-inch wide, creating diamond-shaped pieces. Brush with the remaining butter. Bake in a 400 F degree oven for 5 minutes, then turn down the heat to 325 F degrees and bake for approximately 40 minutes, until evenly browned.

During the last 30 minutes of baking, prepare the honey syrup by combining all the syrup ingredients in a sauce pan big enough to bring them to a boil, and boil for exactly 10 minutes.

Remove the baked baklava from the oven, and pour syrup evenly over it immediately. Allow it to cool to room temperature and enjoy!

Protein: 6% 49 kcal. Fat: 64% 529 kcal. Carbs: 30% 254 kcal

OUR FURRY K⁹ FRIENDS

VANILLA DOG BISCUITS

VANILLA DOG BISCUITS

- 1¼ cup whole wheat flour
- 1¼ cup brown rice flour
- 1 cup rolled oats, quick or old-fashioned
- 2 large eggs
- 1 cup natural peanut butter, plain or crunchy
- 2 tablespoons dried parsley
- 1 tablespoon vanilla extract
- 2 tablespoons dried mint
- ½ cup cold water, approximately, to make cohesive dough

Preheat the oven to 300 F degrees. In a large bowl, mix together the wheat flour, rice flour, oats, mint and parsley. Add the eggs, peanut butter, and vanilla, stirring until combined. The mixture will be crumbly. Add enough water to bring the dough together. Roll the dough out to ¼-inch and cut into squares or use a cookie cutter, placing it on a baking sheet lined with parchment paper. Bake for 40 to 60 minutes or until they are a dark golden brown and crunchy.

My Ka'hi Pua girl, the sweetest little King Charles Cavalier puppy, still chewing on everything, loves these and so do all of her pals in the hood! Making all of their bodies strong and their breath fresh.

Protein: 15% 10 kcal. Fat: 56% 38 kcal. Carbs: 29% 20 kcal

VANILLA COCKTAILS

Add a drop or two of your powerful homemade vanilla extract
into a snifter of cognac or bourbon. It's absolutely sublime.

HAWAI'IAN VANILLA MAI TAI

- 1 jigger light Kauai rum
- ½ jigger Grand Marnier
- ½ jigger Frangelico
- ½ jigger dark rum
- 2 jiggers unsweetened pineapple juice
- 2 jigger orange juice
- Squeeze juice of 1/2 lime and zest
- ¼ teaspoon vanilla extract
- Pinch of bitters

Combine all of the ingredients into a shaker and mix well, and serve over ice with an orchid. Watch out, this is powerful!

HAWAI'IAN VANILLA PUNA-HOU ROCKY ROAD

- 1 jigger Maui vodka
- ½ jigger chocolate liqueur
- ½ jigger macadamia nut liqueur
- ¼ jigger amaretto
- ¼ teaspoon vanilla extract

Mix with club soda, twist of lime or lilikoi over ice.
Don't drive on any road after this one!

MORE OR LEZ

- 1 jigger cognac
- 1 jigger Kauai Kahlua (coffee liqueur)
- 1 jigger amaretto
- ¼ teaspoon vanilla extract

Combine together, and serve in a snifter or over ice.

Came up with this one when I was singing jazz in Waikiki, enjoy!

VANILLA CREAM SODA

- 1 12-oz bottle of club soda or seltzer
- 1 jigger vodka
- 1 tablespoon vanilla simple syrup to taste
- (half sugar, half water cooked down)
- ½ teaspoon vanilla extract

Add together, and serve over ice. Refreshing!

Any of these can be made into mock-tails by removing the alcohol, and because vanilla extract is used in a ¼-teaspoon volume, a very low quantity—and is in much of our food—it should be safe for those who don't drink. But if it's a problem, the vanilla extract can be made with glycerin.

ACKNOWLEDGEMENT

Michael Koa was born at 4:30 a.m. on March 6th, 1988, (same day as Michelangelo and it was my choice for his name) four weeks early and through emergency c-section. He was sceptic with listeria, a rare, deadly bacterial infection that causes fetal demise. From the moment he came into this world, he was at risk, with doctors telling me he wasn't likely to survive. We were both septic and hospitalized, he was in the neonatal intensive care unit at Kapiolani hospital in Honolulu and they wouldn't let me see him or touch him. I refused to sleep or cooperate, and wouldn't accept this fate. It took five long days and nights before they finally allowed me to see and hold my precious newborn son and we had an instantaneous bond. We were aching for each other, however it took almost a month for him to be released to go home.

As a toddler, he was completely fascinated with airplanes and it was one of his first words, second to mama, of course. He learned all of the names and history of the different aircraft and became a mascot of a nearby private (Dillingham) airport where we'd spent hours watching them take off and land. All the pilots there adored him and would take him flying in gliders, bi-planes, all sorts of aircraft, teaching him the ropes, for they all knew he was destined to be a pilot. At six years old, he was invited to co-pilot a Gulfstream IV, he was so excited.

And he did get his wings...

Later on we realized he had perfect pitch and could play by ear, so that he was able to sit down and play any instrument and any piece of music that he wanted. He played trombone in the symphonic orchestra, often first seat and also in the marching band in high school at Punahou.

He'd established himself early on as a talented photographer and videographer with a special interest in documentaries. He had great compassion and empathy for all things living, always protecting his friends from the bullies. He was a gentle, loving old soul in a young man's body.

His life long passion and sport became skateboarding and he was darn good at it, known far and wide for his talents. He was so good at skateboarding that he had all the tricks and flips down. And at the same time, he was able to hold the video camera steady, filming professional skateboarders, while skateboarding himself. At sixteen he was hired by a local surf and skateboard company to film their professional skaters. Surely he was smiling down in 2020, when skateboarding became an Olympic sport. After high school he went on to receive his degree in digital arts at the University of Oregon and was well on his way to a wonderful future.

He was brilliant and humble, blushing at attention he received, with a bright smile that lit up any room and warmed any dark heart. Pure Aloha with a true zest for life, and so incredibly handsome. Obviously a very proud mother.

We had such great times traveling around the world together, testing food all along the way. Not realizing at the time, how incredibly precious these fleeting moments would be to me, the sweet memories that I will hold near and dear to my heart, for the rest of my days.

Writing this book has been a cathartic experience for me. I am a better person because of him. He touched my life and my heart in such deep profound ways, as he did for so many others, along his path.

I am forever grateful to God that I was chosen to be his Mom, if only for a brief moment in time. Mahalo nui loa ke Akua,

Aloha nui loa mio Michelangelo.

CPSIA information can be obtained
at www.ICGtesting.com
Printed in the USA
JSHW041928280223
38327JS00014B/434

9 781977 257314